# THE COMPLETE GUIDE TO

# BEHAVIOURAL CHANGE FOR SPORT AND FITNESS PROFESSIONALS

# THE COMPLETE GUIDE TO
# BEHAVIOURAL CHANGE FOR SPORT AND FITNESS PROFESSIONALS

**Sarah Bolitho, Debbie Lawrence and Elaine McNish**

**Note**
Whilst every effort has been made to ensure that the content of this book is as technically accurate and as sound as possible, neither the author nor the publishers can accept responsibility for any injury or loss sustained as a result of the use of this material.

Published by Bloomsbury Publishing Plc
50 Bedford Square
London WC1B 3DP
www.bloomsbury.com

Copyright © 2012 Sarah Bolitho, Debbie Lawrence and Elaine McNish

ISBN 978 1 4081 6067 1

A CIP catalogue record for this book is available from the British Library.

**Acknowledgements**
Cover photograph © Shutterstock
Illustrations by David Gardner, except Figure 6.3 © Shutterstock; photo for Figure 2.1 © Shutterstock
Designed by James Watson
Commissioned by Charlotte Croft
Edited by Nick Ascroft

This book is produced using paper that is made from wood grown in managed, sustainable forests. It is natural, renewable and recyclable. The logging and manufacturing processes conform to the environmental regulations of the country of origin.

Typeset in 10.75 on 14pt Adobe Caslon by Saxon Graphics Ltd, Derby

Printed and bound in Great Britain by CPI Group (UK) Ltd, Croydon CR0 4YY

# // CONTENTS

# FOREWORD

The message that increased physical activity leads to improved public health has long been understood by fitness professionals but it is only relatively recently that the medical profession has embraced the concept of 'exercise as medicine' for a wide variety of chronic health problems.

However, for both trainers and doctors, there is still the considerable hurdle of motivation to overcome before clients/patients are able to reap the benefits of such programmes.

This excellent book addresses these concerns very specifically, presenting a clear and easy-to-follow guide to the recognition of motivational problems and providing a series of simple strategies designed to overcome them, thus ensuring that the maximum possible number of people are able to enter and – even more importantly – maintain, a physical activity programme.

Written by three very experienced authors with backgrounds in personal training, coaching and teaching at the highest level, *The Complete Guide to Behavioural Change for Sport and Fitness Professionals* should become required reading for anyone trying to persuade – often reluctant – individuals not only that exercise is a very effective way of both treating and preventing poor health but that it can be great fun too!

Dr Colin Crosby MA (Oxon) FFSEM (UK)
FFSEM (I) MB BS (Lond) LRCP MRCS
Consultant in sport and exercise medicine
Medical Director, Department of Sport and
Exercise Medicine, The Garden Hospital,
London

# ACKNOWLEDGEMENTS

Sarah Bolitho

I want to say thank you to the many people I have worked with and learned from over the years and to all my clients who have taught me that there is no 'one size fits all' when it comes to making lasting and positive changes to lifestyle behaviours. Special thanks must go to Vicky Hatch, Alan McPhee and Colin Crosby who have always challenged my thinking and helped me see the wood through the trees! There are too many others to name individually but I hope you know who you are and how much you have helped me in my career and life.

Thanks are also due to Elaine and Debbie for their knowledge and experience and to everyone at Bloomsbury Sport who continue to give me the opportunity to write about my favourite subjects.

Here's to lasting change!

Debbie Lawrence

I am truly thankful that my career and my life offer many opportunities to write, teach, share what I know and learn from others.

Special thanks to: my partner Joe for his ongoing love, support and uplifting spirit; my mum, dad, brother and sisters for their contribution to my life; my therapy teachers and mentors – Sheila Norris, Graz Amber, Mike Berry, Marilia Angove; my clients who are always a source of inspiration; my friends for sharing many stories and journeys, especially Ms Alex Carr; and my heroes of the therapy world – Carl Rogers, Carl Jung, Fritz Perls, Irvine Yalom, Eric Berne (to name but a few).

Thanks also to my co-authors Sarah and Elaine for sharing their knowledge and to the team at Bloomsbury who are always supportive and work to make ideas and projects happen.

Thank you, thank you, thank you!

Wishing all good things.

Elaine McNish

I want to thank the people who have helped contribute to the development of this book. My Mum who has an innate skill for building rapport and supporting people – hopefully I have picked up some of her natural talents. My Dad for giving me a lifelong love of sport and physical activity and the drive to want to make a difference. My sister and brother, Pauline and David, for being there when I needed them. My work colleagues who have supported my career and enabled my learning over the years. My clients for allowing me to work with them and help develop my skills. My wonderful friends for listening and helping me shape my ideas while I wrote this book, and their unflinching support over the years. Sarah and Debbie who gave me the opportunity to write my first book and have supported me through the creative process. And finally Bloomsbury for giving me the opportunity to write about this vital topic.

Thank you all.

# INTRODUCTION

The health, or ill health, of the nation is an ongoing topic of discussion and debate with many different theories and ideas of how negative behaviours impact on health and subsequently burden the UK's National Health Service. Promoting positive health behaviours is an important factor in improving the health of the nation and the National Institute of Health and Clinical Excellence (NICE) have issued public health guidance on behaviour change, which is a welcome move.

Fitness professionals, health-care professionals and sports coaches have an important role in both initiating and supporting long-term changes in lifestyle behaviours to promote health, and are ideally placed to provide information and strategies for short-term changes that lead to lasting changes.

The main purpose of this book is to provide a reference guide for professionals from the health and fitness industry, particularly those working at Levels 3 and 4 of the qualifications framework. It is also suitable for undergraduates and postgraduates pursuing any sport or health-related activity course and those working to promote activity in community settings. It would be useful for anyone wishing to increase personal knowledge of behaviour change and motivation. It covers many of the Level 3 and 4 requirements detailed within the Health and Fitness National Occupational Standards and the Qualifications Framework pertaining to behaviour change and motivation for working with clients. This includes individuals with health-risk factors who need support to become active, referred clients, recreational and amateur athletes who want to change their lifestyle or mental attitude in order to improve their performance and personal training clients who are unsure about how to make lasting changes to their lifestyle.

# SECTION ONE

## UNDERPINNING KNOWLEDGE

### INTRODUCTION

Despite the best effort of both the fitness and sports industries, participation rates for adults have remained consistently low over the past 20 years. One of the reasons for this may be the lack of understanding among sport and fitness professionals of how to effectively motivate and encourage people to be physically active. It is therefore important that practitioners (exercise instructors, sports coaches or health professionals) find out more about how to help people make changes to their lifestyle and behaviour; and this in turn involves learning about and applying strategies to assist behaviour change. With the array of models and methods in existence, it is easy to become confused and unclear on what is best practice when working with clients to support behaviour change. There is no 'one size fits all' approach and often an integrated approach, which considers the concepts within a range of models and theories, will need to be applied.

It is important for practitioners to have an understanding of the many different models available and, more importantly, an awareness of how these can be used, adapted and applied when working with clients. It is the aim of this book to help with that, and to provide guidance for helping clients change lifestyle behaviours. The main focus is on physical activity, however, the theory and techniques discussed can be applied to any area where change is required.

# // CHANGE

1

The aim of this chapter is to provide an introduction and outline of change and behaviour change, including:

- A definition of change.
- An overview of comfort zones.
- A clear outline of the difference between coaching or helping with change and counselling.
- An overview of some of the professional boundaries for exercise professionals.

## WHAT IS CHANGE?

One thing that all people can be certain of through life is that things change. From birth to death, we grow and develop and our lives, circumstances and relationships with others change. Whether we are consciously aware or not, any decision we make has a significant role in the way our own lives evolve and how we behave, even if that decision is not to do anything.

Occasionally, people may find themselves in a situation, possibly brought on by a lifestyle behaviour, that causes discomfort or unhappiness (pain) or they may want to move forward to a better place (pleasure) but they may feel stuck where they are and need help and support to start or continue a change process. They may feel the need to change as something has been brought to their attention by someone else, for example, a GP diagnosing a health risk, a friend becoming ill or a sports coach identifying a need to improve performance. Changes in life circumstances such as the loss of a job/redundancy, break-up of a relationship, etc., may make them question or examine their current situation. Alternatively, they may feel intrinsically that something is not right for them (e.g. they may feel unhappy or displeased with a situation, a habit and/or performance). At these times, a decision to make changes will arise.

When the need for change arises, an individual may want to move forward but feel blocked by internal factors (e.g. I will not be able to do this, I am scared, etc.) or by external factors (e.g. they feel that change is imposed upon them and they want to stay where they are, in the comfort zone they know). It is then that people make the choice to either stay with the known or take steps to help them move forward into the unknown.

For many people, change can be a scary process. Some people may ask for help, support and advice from friends or family, while some may seek professional guidance from a counsellor, instructor, life coach or sports coach to help them overcome the obstacles or barriers that prevent them from moving in the direction they would like to move.

Every person has comfort zones (see Figure 1.1). The inner zone consists of things that we are confident about and comfortable doing – it is known and safe. The outer zone is unknown or may consist of things that we do not like doing or think we are not capable of and feels unsafe, arousing fear and anxiety. An individual may construct and apply these zones consciously or unconsciously to protect themselves – and how they see themselves – and this will affect their behaviour. For example, a person may think that they are not sporty if they had a bad experience of PE as a child. They will therefore see sport as being outside their comfort zone, associating it with feelings of stress or anxiety.

Comfort zones are (and often need to be) protected by boundaries – even talking about some subjects (e.g. where to make changes) may be off-limit to certain people at certain times of their lives.

This means that at times these zones need respecting because they are keeping the person safe. At other times, they need challenging as they may be blocking growth, development and change. The person may hold self-limiting beliefs that are preventing them from expanding or stepping outside their comfort zone and it is the role of the counsellor, coach or helper to challenge these beliefs in an empathetic and appropriate manner, to assist the client in becoming 'unstuck'.

There may be a need to challenge not just the comfort zone but also the perception of the world as people seek to protect their 'map' of the world

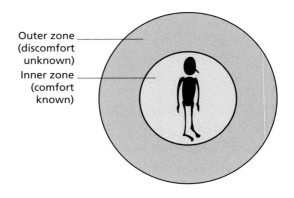

Outer zone (discomfort unknown)

Inner zone (comfort known)

**Figure 1.1** Comfort zones

and find information to confirm it, which can lead to a resistance towards change. This needs care as unskilled challenging, challenging prematurely or sometimes self-challenging without an alternative perspective or guide can reinforce the barriers and prevent forward movement and change.

As the old saying goes, 'when the person is ready, the teacher will appear'. The teacher may not always be a person, but might be an event that enables the potential for self-knowledge and for the development of greater awareness to the inner resources and strengths we all possess.

Life will present us with continuous lessons and teachers. We all have the potential to live life to the full and to learn from all experiences – but we must be willing to make changes and look outside our comfort zones.

If we don't change, we don't grow. If we do not grow, we are not really living. Growth demands a temporary surrender of security. It may mean giving up familiar but limiting patterns, safe but unrewarding work, values no longer believed in, relationships that have lost their meaning. As Dostoevsky put it, 'taking a new step, uttering a new word, is what people fear most'. The real fear should be of the opposite course. (Gail Sheehy, in Orlick 1980)

# COUNSELLING AND COACHING

The terms counselling and coaching are often used synonymously and the differentiation between the two practices is a topic that is open for much discussion and debate in both counselling and coaching circles, and in the wider field of behaviour change.

A lack of consensus among professional circles makes it even more difficult for the lay person to distinguish between the two practices, so the aim of this section is to provide a brief introduction to both counselling and coaching, and identify some of the ways in which they may, or may not, be similar or different. It is not possible to capture the fullness of how individual counsellors and coaches work with their clients, so only a generalised overview is provided here. Some examples of applications of coaching in different settings are

explored in Section 3 with examples of coaching and counselling case studies.

It should be noted that reading this section will not provide the reader with the skills or knowledge required to practise as either a professional counsellor or professional coach; it will simply introduce the two practices. Individuals who are interested in training as either a counsellor or a coach and working with clients professionally to help lifestyle/behaviour change are advised to contact the professional organisations listed in this section.

## PERCEPTION, PROCESS AND PRACTICE

One key difference between the two practices may be how they are perceived, both by professionals and by the layperson (that is, the service providers and the service users). People may choose to work with a coach or counsellor for a variety of different personal or professional reasons. However, there is arguably less stigma attached to working with a coach, than working with a counsellor.

| Table 1.1 | Counselling or coaching |
|---|---|
| **Coaching or counselling** | **Purpose** |
| Sports | To explore and develop sporting performance |
| Life | To explore and develop personal and professional goals – work-life balance |
| Business | To explore and develop performance in business or within an organisation |
| Career | To explore and develop career options and choices |
| Lifestyle | To explore and support lifestyle change (alcohol, smoking, exercise, diet, etc.) |
| Relationship | To explore and develop relationships |
| Grief | To explore experiences of loss or bereavement |
| Mental health | To explore feelings (e.g. sadness, anger, etc.) that are of unknown origin (e.g. not linked to a specific life event) |

## COUNSELLING

Working with a counsellor is often misunderstood by those who do not understand the process. It can be assumed that people speak with a counsellor only when they have a problem or are experiencing a struggle coping with a life event (grief, unemployment, relationship break-up, etc.) and are unable to manage.

Someone who discloses that they are speaking with a counsellor may be subject to certain assumptions and judgements. Their decision to speak with a counsellor may raise concerns that they are weak or unable to cope with or manage their problems or struggles (if indeed they have any); or that they may have deeper, unresolved psychological issues to deal with. While there may be a grain of truth in these assumptions, passing a judgement is unhelpful.

The reality is that people often choose to speak with a counsellor for a variety of reasons, which may include help with solving problems and resolving issues and conflicts, but may equally include personal growth and enhancement. Both coaching and counselling are growth-enhancing and help with relationships. Any person who is able to ask for help and support, whether to manage a struggle or explore how to achieve a goal, is showing a sign of their own self-worth and is respecting their own skills and strength.

Other styles of counselling will have a different focus. Counsellors who work within the psychodynamic paradigm will focus on helping the client to explore how their present issues may be connected to the past. They will help the client to gain insight and understanding of the potential origins of any specific issues, with the view of healing any unresolved psychological issues in the present. Coaching and some other forms of

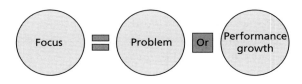

**Figure 1.2** Focus of counselling

counselling (such as cognitive behavioural therapy (CBT), etc.) may reflect back on and consider the past, but this will usually be as a way of discovering a block; any deeper insight and understanding of that block would not usually be the focus of the work (see Figure 1.2).

### Counselling definitions

The British Association for Counselling & Psychotherapy (BACP 2011) describes counselling and psychotherapy as 'umbrella terms that cover a broad range of talking therapies, delivered by trained practitioners who work with people over a short or long term to help them bring about effective change or enhance their wellbeing'.

Counselling is primarily a helping relationship, usually undertaken by a professional from the helping services (counsellor, psychiatrist, counselling psychologist), who uses different interventions to explore the individuals psychological processes, with the goal of helping the individual to make their own choices and decisions, and take responsibility for these choices and decisions (Nelson-Jones 1997: 3) (see Figure 1.3).

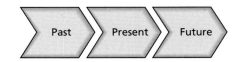

**Figure 1.3** Counselling model

Professional counsellors can be differentiated from individuals who use counselling skills (formally or informally), because they have been formally trained, have explored a range of counselling theories and hold qualifications to work in their chosen field.

## Training and approaches

There are a number of different approaches to counselling and psychotherapy. An overview of some of these approaches appears in Figure 1.4 (adapted from Sanders 1997: 15)

More information on the organisations that provide training in the different areas is available from the BACP website listed at the end of this section.

## Counselling ethics

Most professional counsellors register with bodies, such as the BACP, and work within their ethical framework. Counsellors who are registered with the BACP agree to respect the fundamental values of counselling and psychotherapy (BACP 2010: 1), which include:

- Respecting human rights and dignity.
- Ensuring the integrity of practitioner and client relationships.
- Enhancing the quality of professional knowledge and its application.
- Alleviating personal distress and suffering.
- Fostering a sense of self that is meaningful to the person(s) concerned.

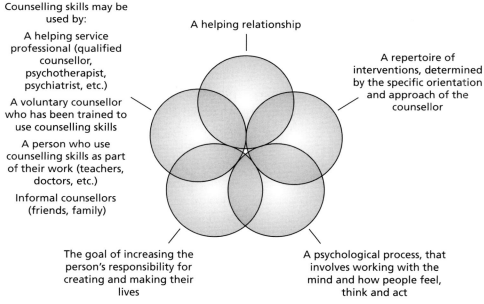

Counselling skills may be used by:

A helping service professional (qualified counsellor, psychotherapist, psychiatrist, etc.)

A voluntary counsellor who has been trained to use counselling skills

A person who use counselling skills as part of their work (teachers, doctors, etc.)

Informal counsellors (friends, family)

A helping relationship

A repertoire of interventions, determined by the specific orientation and approach of the counsellor

The goal of increasing the person's responsibility for creating and making their lives

A psychological process, that involves working with the mind and how people feel, think and act

*NB: These approaches are not exhaustive. They are included to provide an example of the many different approaches to counselling and psychotherapy.*

**Figure 1.4** Overview of approaches

- Increasing personal effectiveness.
- Enhancing the quality of relationships between people.
- Appreciating the variety of human experience and culture.
- Striving for fair and adequate provision of counselling and psychotherapy services.

These values underpin and inform the principles that guide registered practitioners' work and reflect the BACP's (2010: 2) ethical commitment to counselling practice.

The key principles of counselling and psychotherapy include:

- Being trustworthy: honouring the trust placed in the practitioner.
- Autonomy: respect for the client's right to be self-governing.
- Beneficence: a commitment to promoting the client's well-being.
- Non-maleficence: a commitment to avoiding harm to the client.
- Justice: the fair and impartial treatment of all clients and the provision of adequate services.
- Self-respect: fostering the practitioners self-knowledge and care for self.

Personal moral qualities to which counsellors are recommended to aspire (BACP 2010: 4) include:

- Empathy: being able to communicate understanding of another person's experience from that person's perspective (walking in the person's shoes).
- Sincerity: a personal commitment to what is professed and what is done (walking the talk).

- Integrity: commitment to being moral in dealings with others, personal straight-forwardness, honesty and coherence.
- Resilience: the capacity to work with the client's concerns without being personally diminished.
- Respect: showing appropriate esteem to others and their understanding of themselves.
- Humility: ability to assess accurately and acknowledge one's own strengths and weaknesses.
- Competence: effective deployment of the skills and knowledge needed to do what is required.
- Fairness: the consistent application of appropriate criteria to inform decisions and actions.
- Wisdom: possession of sound judgement that informs practice.
- Courage: the capacity to act in spite of fears, risks and uncertainty.

The BACP provides the framework to assist practitioners when they encounter situations where they are faced with competing obligations that may challenge their decision-making and commitment to working ethically. Rather than retreating from ethical analysis, practitioners are encouraged to work with courage and consideration of the variety of issues they may face (BACP 2010: 4).

As part of their professional and ethical practice, counsellors in practice are required to have their work supervised (usually one hour of supervision per six hours of client work for counsellors in training). The aim of this process is to ensure the counsellor is working within the ethical framework; it also offers the opportunity for the counsellor to reflect on and discuss their work (successes and blocks) and review the therapeutic process and the working alliance/relationship. Supervision is discussed later in this section under the heading 'Professional alliance, relationship and boundaries'.

Sanders (1997: 9) summarises the following *boundaries* to delineate *professional counselling*:

- It is practised by someone who has been designated the role of being a counsellor and who works for a counselling service or in private practice.
- It is practised by a person who is appropriately trained and qualified and registered with a professional body – such as the BACP or the United Kingdom Council for Psychotherapy (UKCP) – and who abides to an appropriate code of ethics.
- The client knows the service being offered by the counsellor is counselling.

## COACHING

Coaching has been a well-established activity in the sporting community for many years. No sports team or athlete would be expected to train without a coach to advise and guide them. In fact, many sports people often work with a number of coaches throughout their career to develop their performance and skill. Coaching is viewed as part of the process for achieving success in a variety of both team and individual sporting events.

Similarly, in the world of business, organisational or executive coaching is becoming a professionally respected tradition. Working with a coach (or mentor) either formally or informally is viewed as important in enhancing an individual's professional growth and development, to help them navigate their way in the professional world.

Executive coaching is an experiential and individualized leader development process that builds a leader's capability to achieve short- and long-term organizational goals. It is conducted through one-on-one and/or group interactions, driven by data from multiple perspectives, and based on mutual trust and respect. The organization, an executive, and the executive coach work in partnership to achieve maximum impact. (Executive Coaching Forum 2008)

More recently, the use of life coaching has been embraced as an approach that can help individuals to clarify their personal goals and manage their personal and professional lives more effectively, and take appropriate action to achieve their goals and create a work-life balance.

Everyone needs help and guidance at some point in their life. An athlete or sports team would be viewed as wise for seeking help from a coach. Similarly, speaking with a coach to build success in business or our career would be deemed a good decision. Likewise, asking for help to support personal growth and processes, whether from a professional counsellor, a professional coach, or indeed even informally via family and friends, is also showing wisdom.

### Coaching definition

Coaching is defined by the International Coaching Federation (ICF) as:

An ongoing partnership that helps clients to produce fulfilling results in their personal and professional lives. Through the process of coaching, clients deepen their learning, improve their performance, and enhance their quality of life. Beginning with the client's desires, coaching uses reporting, exploring, and a consistent commitment to move the client forward. Coaching accelerates the clients' progress by providing greater focus and awareness of choice. Coaching concentrates on where the client is today and what they are willing to do to get where they want to be tomorrow.' (www.coachfederation.org)

## Focus of the work

The focus of coaching is often perceived as being to enhance performance, whereas, the focus of counselling is often perceived as being to manage a problem. Enhancing performance and managing a problem are potentially two sides of the same coin and both counsellors and coaches will address both issues at some point in their work. The outcome for both counselling and coaching will ultimately be to enhance growth and improve performance in the future, despite any potential differences in the focus of the work (see Figure 1.5).

Most coaching practice will explore the present situation and help clients to formulate specific goals they would like to achieve in the future. The focus of the work is on action and moving forward.

## Training and approaches

There are a variety of coaching courses delivered across the UK, each dependant or focused on the field in which the coach seeks to work. Those working in sport should ensure that their course is delivered by a recognised governing body and meet National Occupational standards. Further advice can be gained from Sports Coach UK.

Executive and life coaching is not so well coordinated and there are a number of membership organisations that recognise specific training providers. Some examples include the International Coaching Federation, the European Coaching Institute, the European Mentoring and Coaching Council, and the Association for Coaching. The Institute of Leadership and Management also offers a range of levels of coaching and mentoring qualifications.

Regardless of the organisation, the key approach is that the coach works in partnership with the client to plan the process, and work cooperatively towards meeting the agreed goals. The coach's role is to help the client increase awareness of their behaviour and support them to develop their skills, while encouraging them to take responsibility for action to improve their performance. There are a variety of coaching models and tools available, and the sessions may include the following elements:

- Contracting – this is agreeing how the sessions will operate, the roles and expectations for the sessions alongside key issues such as confidentiality.
- Identification of the areas for development, which may include the use of tools to assess skills and competencies
- Discussion of the identified issue using appropriate questioning and a specific coaching model such as GROW (Goals, Reality, Options, Will and Way forward) or OSKAR (Outcome, Scaling, Know-how and Resources, Affirm and action, Review). These methods will allow the goal to be identified, a discussion of any issues and problem solving, and the development of an action plan.
- The teaching and application of a variety of tools (e.g. leadership, management, time planning, life planning).
- Implementation of actions.
- Review of progress.

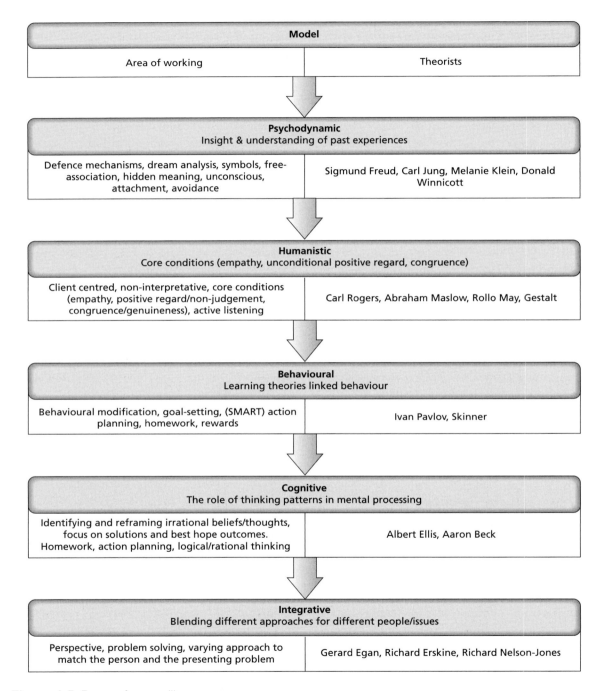

**Figure 1.5** Focus of counselling

In summary, there are differences between counselling and coaching that may not be obvious to the layperson, however, it is often the perception of each that has the most effect as there is still a certain amount of stigma and negative bias attached to counselling while coaching is seen as more positive.

## COMMON GROUND BETWEEN COUNSELLING AND COACHING

There are commonalities between these two approaches that cannot be easily separated.

### Style of working

A key perceived difference or similarity between counselling and coaching may be in the style of working.

Coaching is often viewed as being the more directive and structured approach to working. In sport and in business, a coach may help an individual by challenging them to identify their strengths and recognising areas they need to develop. A coach may use a variety of tools and strategies that the individual can practise on their own (homework).

Similarly, there are some approaches to counselling that also offer a more directive and structured way of working, for example, cognitive behavioural therapy, problem- or solution-focused therapy, time-limited therapy, etc. (NB. Some of the different approaches to counselling and coaching will be introduced later in this chapter and some will be explored further in subsequent chapters).

Counselling is sometimes viewed as being a softer, more tender and nurturing approach to working. However, valuing the individual (positive regard), showing empathy for their position and demonstrating person-centred core values often forms the foundation for both counselling and coaching practice. In particular, motivational interviewing has a strong core essence of person-centred working embedded within practice.

To add further confusion, some counsellors may choose to train as coaches and may choose to name their practice as coaching – perhaps to encourage more people to use their services. Similarly, some coaches may train as counsellors, to enable them to work using practices from other paradigms.

So far, it has proved challenging to differentiate fully between counselling and coaching. There is, in most instances some overlap between the two practices; an overlap that even the professionals who deliver the services can struggle to separate.

### Professional affiliation, training, qualifications and supervision

A key area of difference between the practices of coaching and counselling is within the domain of professional affiliations and the training and qualifications that need to be undertaken in order to perform each role.

Counselling and coaching are usually conducted by individuals who:

- Have been trained to work with clients in different ways (using different methodology, theory and approaches);
- Hold different qualifications and are affiliated and registered with different professional bodies (for counselling, BACP, UKCP; for coaching, Chartered Institute of Professional Development (CIPD), International Coaching Federation (ICF));
- Have different styles of relationships (and boundaries) with their clients and with others (stakeholders, e.g. organisations and sports

team managers, etc.) who may have an investment in the person's achievement and success (i.e. what the person learns from the process and the decisions and choices they make as a consequence of this learning).

Coaches should also work within an ethical framework, which may include working to a recognised code of practice, working with clients appropriate to their skills and making referrals to other professionals when appropriate, and have appropriate insurance. It is recommended that a more experienced professional supervise their work in some way.

The ICF code of ethical practice includes consideration to professional conduct, confidentiality and privacy, avoidance of conflicts of interest and pledging accountability to work within the ICF framework. Some of the other bodies listed also have codes of ethics, for example, the European Mentoring and Coaching Council (EMCC) covers competence, understanding the context, boundary management, integrity and professionalism.

## The working alliance, relationships and boundaries

Another area where some similarities and differences may exist between the working practice of counsellors and coaches is the working alliance and level of relationship.

While sport and exercise professionals may not be working specifically from a coaching or counselling paradigm, it is useful for them to establish the foundations for and boundaries to their work. Sport and exercise professionals should also follow the ethical principles established by their own professional or sports governing bodies.

Most of the aspects discussed in subsequent paragraphs will apply to all helping relationships. In any helping relationship (counsellors, coaches and exercise professionals), the potential for the work and any limitations of the work, including boundaries should be discussed and agreed in the very first session (a working contract). Firm foundations for the work and clear boundaries offer clarity and protection for both helper and client.

## Boundaries

Boundaries provide clarity for both the practitioner and the client. Boundaries clearly assert the limitations of any helping relationship (and there are always limits). These limits are likely to be reflected in the ethical frameworks of the specific professions. Sorting this out in advance is referred to as 'contracting' in coaching and counselling circles and needs to be agreed as the first step in the coaching process.

Areas that require definition of and adherence to clear boundaries for counsellors, coaches and exercise professionals alike include:

- The structure of the work, such as the duration of the contract and an outline of what will happen and when, including timing, frequency and content of sessions.
- The level of relationship and relating, including what can and cannot be worked with, the roles of other professionals in the work, trust and confidentiality issues.
- The process and ways of working, such as the number of contact sessions, any distance work, one-to-one or group, telephone, homework, etc.

- The focus for the work, including what can and cannot be addressed within the agreed time frame and what areas are outside of professional competence and require the involvement of other professionals (exercise professionals should not take on a counselling or coaching role unless they are qualified and specifically employed by the organisation/individual to provide that helping service).
- Other appropriate boundaries, such as payment of fees, policy for cancellation, lateness, etc.

Any practitioner who works without boundaries is increasing their risk of personal stress and burn-out and will be reducing their effectiveness as a practitioner, as well as potentially breaching ethical codes.

## Confidentiality

Confidentiality issues need to be addressed and contracted at the start of the helping relationship. It is usual practice in personal counselling and coaching that what is shared in the room stays in the room; there are no other stakeholders.

The exceptions to this rule in counselling would be that most counsellors and coaches work under the guidance of supervisors and will explore and share their client work (although not client names) with their supervisor. Another exception would be if the individual was believed to be at risk of harming themselves or others; in which case, other persons would need to be contacted. The ethical issue of crossing this boundary and sharing information would need to be contracted explicitly at the start of the relationship.

Another area where an exception may apply is when coaching or counselling is commissioned by a third party, for example, as part of a review or a performance development programme (in business or sporting performance). In these instances, the relationship changes from a two-way process to a three-way process and the practitioner may be required to write reports for an individual's manager or a sports performance director. Once again, an agreement will need to be reached with the client at the very start of the working relationship regarding the information that can be disclosed.

In all helping relationships, honesty, integrity and transparency are essential, if the work is to be positive and meaningful. Furthermore, clarity regarding confidentiality issues is paramount to the level of trust that is established in the relationship.

## Trust

Trust in a relationship is something that usually builds over time. Most people have experienced varying levels of trust in other past relationships and if they have experienced being let down or other negative experiences, then this may affect the helping relationship (see transference, discussed later).

It is natural for most people to need time to build trust. The duration of the work may therefore have an impact on the level of trust that is established. There is potential in a longer-term working relationship for greater trust to be established, while, in shorter-term work, the level of trust that can be established may be limited.

The foundation for the development of trust in any helping relationship is to establish at the very start of the work some clear, ethically sound working principles and boundaries (as listed above) and work consistently within these principles and boundaries.

## Transference

Transference is the displacement of an attitude or emotion from one relationship to another relationship. For example, the feelings and attitudes held for another person (e.g. a parent or parental figure, etc.) may be displaced to the helper (counsellor or coach), the person may be 'idealized, imitated or hated' (Bayne et al 1998: 154).

In psychodynamic counselling, these issues are used to explore early developmental conflicts. In other counselling approaches, potential transference will be challenged, to ensure the counsellor is seen for who they are, rather than who the client believes they are (Bayne et al 1998).

In a coaching relationship, issues of transference are of less concern. The coach may be aware of these issues, but will not work with them directly, thus the boundaries of the relationship can potentially be more flexible. However, there will need to be boundaries and the ethical framework of the professional organisations that the coach is affiliated to will provide this guidance.

Sport and exercise professionals are unlikely to be trained to work with issues of transference, although some may recognise or have experienced the potential dynamic in their relationship with some clients (e.g. the client who wants to be a friend or the client who follows every instruction, by the book, saying 'you told me to'). This is not to say that clients who want to be friends should be rejected or that clients who follow instructions should not. However, it raises the need for sport and exercise professionals to explore their own ethical framework and ways of working, and to consider the need for additional guidance and supervision to manage these issues.

## Self-disclosure

Clients often wish to explore more about their counsellor, coach or exercise professional, which may serve as a method for helping them to build trust.

In a coaching relationship, self-disclosure is less of an ethical and boundary issue; there is more freedom for the coach to reveal certain aspects of themselves. Similarly, for exercise professionals, self-disclosure is less of an ethical issue, however, consideration should be given to the amount of information disclosed, to ensure professional practice.

However, in most counselling approaches, self-disclosure is seen as being an ethical issue and something that needs to be monitored and reflected on in supervision. Different counselling orientations will have different approaches to how they manage requests for self-disclosure. Bayne et al (1998: 155) suggest that, while it is not necessary for the counsellor to answer all questions a client asks, it is equally important not to be evasive or secretive as this may cause mistrust.

Bayne et al (1998: 136) also identify different levels of self-disclosure:

- Historical revelations, which they suggest may be useful for helping clients who struggle to talk about themselves, but should be used with caution.
- Present revelations, which are part of the working relationship (e.g. expressing feelings in the present).
- Non-verbal gestures (facial expressions, etc.), which are inevitable.

The key for self-disclosure in counselling and indeed in any helping relationship is that it should be meaningful, purposeful, 'direct, brief and relevant' (Bayne et al 1998: 136).

## Supervision

It is a requirement by professional counselling bodies in the UK (e.g. BACP) that all practising counsellors participate in regular supervision with a more experienced counsellor/supervisor. The aim of supervision is to ensure the counsellor is working within their ethical framework; and offers the opportunity for the counsellor to reflect on and discuss their work (successes and blocks) and review the therapeutic process and the working alliance/relationship in a professional setting.

While coaches are not required by any professional body to have their work supervised, it is often a recommendation that supervision by a more experienced professional is good practice in most professions.

Similarly, exercise and sport professionals who are working in settings that require them to use their skills to help people make changes to their lifestyle (e.g. exercise referral) may also benefit from supervision of their practice. Some exercise and sport professionals in these settings may feel overwhelmed by some of the information their clients disclose to them. Supervision of their practice would provide an opportunity for them to discuss their work and explore ways of managing information; it would also enable an opportunity to explore and clarify boundaries of their work, in these settings.

## Self-awareness

There is potential in any relationship for people to learn more about themselves, by giving and receiving feedback.

Developing greater self-awareness (including self-esteem and confidence) are a focus within both counselling and coaching. Both practices offer a space for the client to explore and learn more about themselves – who they are, how they see themselves and others, and how others may see them, etc. The amount of exploration and information that clients reveal is often determined by the extent to which they trust the helper (see trust and confidentiality issues, discussed earlier).

In counselling, the level of self-awareness and approach to exploration will to some extent be determined by the orientation of the counsellor. Some counselling approaches explore deeper issues (psychodynamic approaches), others explore opposing aspects of the self using experiments such as the Empty Chair; other approaches explore 'existential' issues – life, death, spirituality (e.g. transpersonal approaches and psychosynthesis); while others focus primarily on thinking and mental processes (cognitive behavioural therapy).

There may be times within some counselling approaches and most coaching situations where the counsellor or coach will challenge the clients and hold up a mirror for the client to see themselves. Challenging may also include providing the client with feedback. For example, a client may believe they are fearful, so the counsellor or coach may highlight instances where the client has been courageous.

The purpose of challenging is: to raise awareness of something that may be at the edge of the person's current awareness; to explore mismatches between their verbal and non-verbal signals (e.g. a client may tell a sad story and smile); to encourage ownership of an issue (e.g. exploring self-defeating behaviours or irrational thoughts);

or explore the dynamics of the relationship (usually only in counselling) or patterns of behaving (Bayne et al 1998).

Any challenge should be tentative and ideally, the client should be encouraged to self-challenge, e.g. 'You say you are scared but you also say you have done this and this?' Any resistance to challenges should be accepted and clients should always be given time to respond. Challenge should also focus on 'strengths and resources, rather than weaknesses and deficits' (Bayne et al 1998: 23) and any defensive emotions can be sensitively explored. In all instances where a coach or counsellor challenges a client, there will need to be a high level of trust.

## Feedback

The need to offer feedback in counselling and coaching should always be carefully considered and thought through and permission to offer feedback should be sought from the person before it is given (e.g. by asking 'can I offer you some feedback on what I notice or hear?').

Feedback should always be helpful and descriptive and focus on a specific behaviour and what is seen or heard, rather than being generalised or making a judgement. Feedback should be given on something that is within the person's ability to control, something they can actually do something about, and should always be respectful and assertive. For example, 'I notice that you arrived five minutes late for your session today', rather than, 'you are always late'. The first statement describes something specific the person has noticed, whereas, the second statement is generalised and passing a judgement.

There is an art to providing effective feedback. Counsellors are provided with many opportunities during their training to practise giving and receiving feedback, so that they are skilled in this practice.

Through the practice of challenging and receiving feedback from others and disclosing more about themselves to others during their training, counsellors (and subsequently, their clients) develop greater self-awareness (see the 'unknown self' quadrant in Johari's Window, Figure 1.6).

## Delivery

Delivery of coaching can often be more flexible than counselling and use a variety of modalities (email, telephone, social media, meetings, etc.) and without too much concern for how this may infringe on boundaries, etc.

However, within counselling, the ethics and boundaries of different ways of working will need to be clearly explored and the boundaries of these alternative working methods established (e.g. timing on sessions, how and when they happen, etc.). All counselling practice needs to be considered with regard to the ethical framework.

## Power

In both counselling and coaching relationships, there is to some extent an imbalance of power in the relationship; clients are asking for help and may be vulnerable. The counsellor or coach often has more knowledge, or is seen as being an authority or expert. The client discloses more information about themselves than the counsellor or coach, and the work usually takes place in an environmental setting that is familiar and known to the counsellor or coach.

In any situation where there is an imbalance of power (real or perceived), there is also a potential

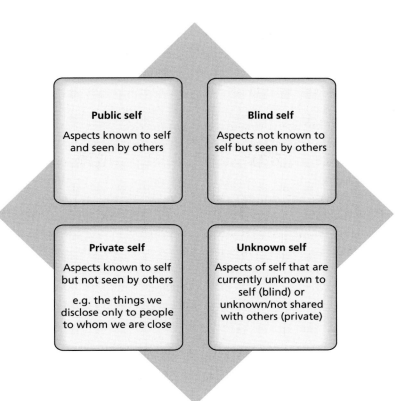

**Figure 1.6** Johari's Window

for misuse or abuse of power, and this can provide a barrier to the development of trust. Once again, these issues are something that counsellors would explore in supervision and, if these issues are seen as barriers to work, then they may be addressed with the client as part of the work. Most counselling practice would aim to level any power imbalance by being aware of any actual or perceived power differences, listening to the client and encouraging and supporting client responsibility and autonomy, which may include renegotiating ways of working if necessary (Bayne et al 1998: 114).

## Prejudice

Prejudice can be defined as thinking, feeling, perceiving or behaving in a way that favours or disfavours a specific person or group of people (Sanders 1997). Areas for discrimination include gender, age, ethnicity, sexual orientation, disability, social class and religion.

There is no place for prejudice in any helping profession. Any potential areas of prejudice or pre-existing perceptions, e.g. all fat people are lazy, should be explored and addressed. The professional must start from a a neutral position and 'walk in the client's shoes'.

## Feelings/emotional work

Working with feelings and emotions directly (up close and personal, as opposed to talking about them in a distant and unemotional way) is not usually the focus of coaching. However, within many counselling approaches (person-centred, psychodynamic, inner child, relational approaches, transactional analysis, Gestalt) working directly with feelings and experiencing of feelings is encouraged to enable greater connection.

Working with feelings demands emotional literacy from the counsellor and within their training they will be exposed to different ways of meeting emotions, e.g. listening to others speak about their feelings or witnessing someone expressing a feeling (crying, etc.), thinking or talking about their own feelings and/or expressing their own feelings (Sanders 1997: 47). Some counselling schools require counsellors to participate in their own personal therapy to enable them to develop this connection.

Awareness of feelings and connection to feelings may be the bedrock for developing empathy with clients. To listen sensitively means being sensitive to the whole person and feelings and emotions are part of every person. Any lack of connection to their own feelings or fear of experiencing or expressing feelings (from the counsellor or coach) may provide a blind spot in awareness and limit the extent of help that can be provided (Sanders 1997: 47).

Sanders (1997: 46), quotes the American psychologist Carl Rogers, who writes: 'If I can form a helping relationship to myself – if I can be sensitively aware of and acceptant toward my own feelings – then the likelihood is so great that I can form a helping relationship toward another.'

Ultimately, both counselling and coaching are helping relationships. In most instances, the work is contracted between two people (client and counsellor or coach) and the information discussed between them should remain confidential (see Figure 1.7).

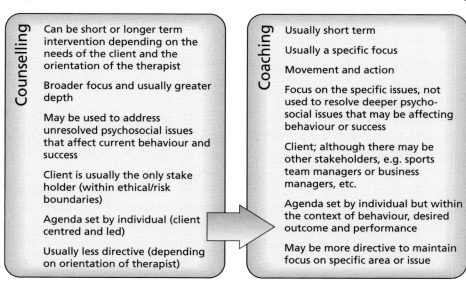

| Counselling | Coaching |
|---|---|
| Can be short or longer term intervention depending on the needs of the client and the orientation of the therapist | Usually short term |
| Broader focus and usually greater depth | Usually a specific focus |
| May be used to address unresolved psychosocial issues that affect current behaviour and success | Movement and action |
| Client is usually the only stake holder (within ethical/risk boundaries) | Focus on the specific issues, not used to resolve deeper psycho-social issues that may be affecting behaviour or success |
| Agenda set by individual (client centred and led) | Client; although there may be other stakeholders, e.g. sports team managers or business managers, etc. |
| Usually less directive (depending on orientation of therapist) | Agenda set by individual but within the context of behaviour, desired outcome and performance |
| | May be more directive to maintain focus on specific area or issue |

**Figure 1.7** Counselling or coaching?

The practitioner should reflect empathy, warmth and genuine interest in the person and see the person they are helping as their equal (not acting as expert). They should accept the person (non-judgement) and the person should be able to discuss any subject openly and honestly and be heard (the counsellor/coach shows empathy and works towards seeing things from the person's perspective).

The helping relationship should encourage self-exploration of thoughts, feelings, behaviours, etc., that will help the individual to identify their own inner resources and lead them towards self-determined change (Russell et al, in Sanders 1997: 3).

Counsellors and coaches may work from different paradigms and within different ethical frameworks, but the outcome of the work is to help another person manage the process of change and gain confidence to act, behave and live in a manner that is congruent with *their own* inner thoughts and feelings.

### Boundaries

Exercise professionals who are working in a helping or guiding role need to very clear about the boundaries of that role and should follow the guidance provided by the Register of Exercise Professionals (REPs), while sports coaches will be bound by the code of conduct of their governing body.

It is important that those without professional training and qualifications should not cross the boundary into another profession. They may use counselling-style skills in their practice, such as active listening (this would be essential for any helping role) and reflecting empathy and non-judgement (core conditions) to be of help to the person. However, they would not be qualified to use many of the other techniques and tools that counsellors and coaches may use – some of which may have a significant impact on an individual's psyche, which professional coaches and counsellors can appreciate and respect.

Even if the exercise professional or sports coach has trained and qualified as a counsellor or coach, they are not usually contracted (employed or freelance/self-employed) to work using a combined role or approach. The roles are distinct. It would be unethical to start practising counselling when contracted to work as an exercise professional and vice versa. Counselling is only counselling when it is a contracted arrangement that is agreed and negotiated with the person requesting this help.

A further consideration would be professional insurance. To practise as a counsellor or coach, individuals need to have professional insurance to protect their work in this area and insurance will only be provided by specific insurance companies, who have seen the qualifications to validate the person's qualifications to work in this area.

The best guidance for exercise professionals would be 'if in doubt, leave it out'. Individuals who have a particular interest in working in a counselling or coaching – or sports psychology – role should seek additional professional training and qualifications by contacting the professional organisations listed in this chapter.

## The counsellor

I see the person as the best expert on themselves and the best thing I can do is to build a relationship with them by listening without judgement (that is, being aware of, and putting aside any judgements that may arise). I offer a genuine warmth for what they bring and an empathy for the feelings they present (core conditions). I may within a session, ask a person if they want to explore something further and I may use different tools and techniques. The way I work with the person is often based on a felt sense of what I feel may be helpful. The client leads the way, I am a resource, I have strengths, I have limitations and I continue to learn. I have participated for a number of years in personal therapy and when practising as a counsellor I respect the ethical framework and value supervision.

Debbie Lawrence (postgraduate diploma in integrative counselling)

## The coach

I see my role as a coach (executive) to support clients in reaching their full potential. I seek to do this do this by creating a safe space for the clients to talk and think – in effect giving them a mental time out. My aim is to understand their perspective then sensitively challenge some of their thinking so that they gain a 360-degree view of the world. By developing this awareness, clients are able to create more choices for themselves and find a course of action that suits their needs. I find that I learn something new from each session I undertake, as each client is different and I am continually looking for new tools and ways of working to improve my coaching skills.

Elaine McNish (ILM level 7 certificate in Executive Coaching and Leadership Mentoring and NLP coach)

## The referral practitioner

Working in referral often means working with clients who have just found out that their health is at risk or poor due to lifestyle, genetic or other factors. They have also been told to exercise – which they may not have done since school so are feeling doubly nervous.

My first priority is to find out what the client expects from the session, from me and/or from activity and to explore that before doing any screening or assessment. This helps build rapport and is essential in helping them feel comfortable and secure so that they are honest about their fears and expectations. My aim is to find out what, if anything, motivates them at this stage and to help them find ways to achieve this and move towards their preferred future.

Sarah Bolitho (postgraduate diploma in exercise and health behaviour)

## KEY POINTS

- Change is a necessary and unavoidable part of life and living.
- It can be hard for an individual to make changes alone.
- Counsellors work with clients to explore ways of making changes to enhance their well-being or health.
- Coaches work with clients to plan and work towards meeting agreed goals.
- Exercise referral professionals work with clients to adopt physical activity as a method of improving health and well-being.
- Sports coaches work with clients to improve sporting or athletic performance.
- Whichever field the practitioner is in, the code of conduct and ethics for that organisation will be the guiding standards for the client/professional relationship.

# THE NEED FOR CHANGE

2

This chapter explores how behaviour patterns develop, why this leads to negative states, what the process of change is and why we need it. The aims of this chapter are to:

- Provide an overview of behaviour and behaviour change.
- State government policy and recommendations for activity and lifestyle.
- Identify how behaviour patterns develop, including intrinsic and extrinsic influences, motivation, environment and learned behaviour.

A brief outline of behaviour change can be seen in 'Autobiography in Five Chapters' by Portia Nelson:

I walk down the street. There is a deep hole in the sidewalk. I fall in. I am lost … I am helpless. It is not my fault. It takes forever to find a way out.

I walk down the same street. There is a deep hole in the sidewalk. I pretend I do not see it. I fall in again. I cannot believe I am in the same place. However, it's not my fault. It still takes a long time to get out.

I walk down the same street. There is a deep hole in the sidewalk. I see it there. I still fall in … it's a habit. My eyes are open. I know where I am. It is my fault. I get out immediately.

I walk down the same street. There is a deep hole in the sidewalk. I walk around it.

I walk down another street. (from Rinpoche 1992)

## WHAT IS LIFESTYLE OR BEHAVIOUR CHANGE?

Lifestyle or behaviour change is literally the process of changing a behaviour or habit and in this context usually involves giving up or swapping a negative or risky habit for a positive one. Changes fall into four broad categories:

1 Cessation: Stopping or giving up a current behaviour that is damaging. For example, giving up smoking.
2 Adoption: Starting a new behaviour that has positive benefits. For example, starting to exercise or be active regularly.

3 Modification: Changing or modifying an existing behaviour to minimise damage or negative impact. For example, cutting back on high alcohol intake to within recommended guidelines.

4 Prevention: Preventing the start of a negative or damaging behaviour. For example, making sure all family meals are healthy to promote future health and good eating habits in your children (Adapted from COI 2009).

Whichever of these categories is relevant, from the perspective of a health professional, the ultimate aim is to help people to make changes they want and/or need towards behaviour that promotes positive health and minimises any health risks associated with negative lifestyles.

## WHY DO WE NEED IT?

The National Institute for Health and Clinical Excellence (NICE) offers guidance aimed at 'behaviour change at population, community and individual levels' (NICE 2007). This states: 'There is overwhelming evidence that changing people's health-related behaviour can have a major impact on some of the largest causes of mortality and morbidity.' The guidance goes on to state that behaviour change interventions targeted at both individuals and communities may have the potential to affect current and future patterns of disease.

The focus of this book is on promoting lifestyle change towards healthy activity and exercise patterns, alongside reducing sedentary or inactive behaviours. This is important as we are an increasingly sedentary nation, and are seeing an alarming rise in associated diseases, such as obesity and diabetes. This is down to a number of complex and interrelated factors, however, the increasing prevalence of inactivity is considered a significant factor.

In the 'old days', activity was an inevitable part of everyday life as most people did something active in their daily life, whether it was walking to school or work, visiting the local shops or going dancing on a Saturday night. There were only three or four television channels to watch and fast food consisted of the local chippy or Chinese takeaway – both of which were occasional treats. Sport was not just something to be watched but to be participated in as kids kicked a ball around outside with their mates, while alcohol was mainly for special occasions and celebrations.

Over the years we have seen a massive change in physical activity behaviour. The increase in labour-saving devices such as automatic washing machines and vacuum cleaners has reduced the level of activity required in household tasks. The increase in car usage together with more out-of-town shopping centres, plus the design of the environment to favour cars over pedestrians has led to a reduction in walking and cycling; concerns about road and community safety have contributed to a reduction in people getting out and about for work, exercise or play. Moreover, we have seen an increase in more sedentary leisure pursuits – such as watching television, playing on games consoles and using computers – combined with changes in eating habits, with greater access to convenient – and usually high fat and sugary – foods.

We have also witnessed the dawn of 'exercisation'. People today have to go out of their way to be active, which has led to the development of structured forms of exercise that attempt to fill the hole left by the reduction in lifestyle activities. More recently, we also have seen the rise in exercise referral or prescription, where exercise is marketed as a treatment for a number of chronic diseases.

So, going back to the original question, why do we need to know about lifestyle behaviour change? For all of the above reasons, plus there is overwhelming evidence that changing people's health-related behaviour can have a major impact on some of the largest causes of mortality and morbidity.

## PHYSICAL ACTIVITY AND PREVENTION OF DISEASE

It has been proved that physical activity plays a key role in risk reduction and disease management. Regularly active individuals have a 30–50 per cent reduction in conditions such as stroke, ischaemic heart disease, cancer, obesity, diabetes and mental health conditions such as depression or dementia, and an inactive person spends 38 per cent more days in hospital and uses significantly more resources than an active person (NHS 2011).

In 2011, the four Chief Medical Officers in the UK published *Start Active Stay Active*. This document provided guidance on the levels of physical activity people should undertake to improve their health (see Table 2.2). The document also highlights the impact of sedentary behaviour on health and advised that both children and adults across the age span should minimise the time they spend sitting down. The new guidance reiterated the importance of physical activity for maintaining good health and in the

| Table 2.1 | Effects of exercise on chronic disease (adapted from NHS 2011) |
|---|---|
| Condition | Effects of exercise therapy |
| Ischaemic heart disease | 35–40 per cent reduction in risk of an event |
| Cerebrovascular disease | Improvement in aerobic capacity, sensorimotor function and cerebrovascular risk factors |
| Hypertension | Decrease in systolic blood pressure by 7.4mmHg and diastolic blood pressure by 5.8mmHg |
| COPD | Improvements in aerobic fitness, quality of life, dyspnoea symptoms, CV risk factors |
| Breast cancer | 50 per cent reduction of relative risk of breast cancer death |
| Bowel cancer | 50 per cent reduction of bowel cancer death |
| Diabetes | 42 per cent reduction in diabetes related mortality 32 per cent reduction in diabetes related complications |
| Impaired glucose tolerance | 42 per cent reduction in risk of developing diabetes |
| Osteoarthritis | Improved aerobic capacity, muscle strength and function, reduced pain and fatigue |
| Osteoporosis | Reduction in falls risk, maintenance of bone mineral density in men and postmenopausal women |
| Depression and anxiety disorders | Effects as good as standard pharmacological treatments for moderate depression |

| **Table 2.2** | **The guidelines for physical activity, adapted from the CMO report** |

## Early years (under 5s)

- Physical activity should be encouraged from birth, particularly through floor-based play and water-based activities in safe environments.

- Children of preschool age who are capable of walking unaided should be physically active daily for at least 180 minutes (3 hours), spread throughout the day.

- All under 5s should minimise the amount of time spent being sedentary (being restrained or sitting) for extended periods (except time spent sleeping).

## Children and young people (5–18 years)

- All children and young people should engage in moderate to vigorous intensity physical activity for at least 60 minutes and up to several hours every day.

- Vigorous intensity activity, including those that strengthen muscle and bone, should be incorporated at least three days a week.

- All children and young people should minimise the time spent being sedentary (sitting) for extended periods.

## Adults (19–64 years)

- Adults should aim to be active daily. Over a week, activity should add up to at least 150 minutes (2 1/2 hours) of moderate intensity activity in bouts of 10 minutes or more – one way to approach this is to do 30 minutes at least five days per week.

- Alternatively comparable benefits can be achieved through 75 minutes of vigorous activity spread across the week or a moderate and vigorous intensity activity.

- Adults should also undertake activity to improve muscle strength on at least two days a week.

- All adults should minimise the time spent being sedentary (sitting) for extended periods.

## Older adults (65+ years)

- Older adults who participate in any physical activity benefit gain some health benefits, including maintenance of good physical and cognitive function. Some physical activity is better than none and more physical activity provides greater health benefits.

- Older adults should aim to be active daily. Over a week, activity should add up to at least 150 minutes (2 1/2 hours) of moderate intensity activity in bouts of 10 minutes or more – one way to approach this is to do 30 minutes at least five days per week.

- For those who are already active at moderate intensity, comparable benefits can be achieved through 75 minutes of vigorous activity spread across the week or a moderate and vigorous intensity activity.

- Older adults at risk of falls should incorporate physical activity to improve balance and coordination on at least two days per week.

- All older adults should minimise the time spent being sedentary (sitting) for extended periods.

prevention of chronic disease and improving mental health. The document called for urgent action to improve public health through encouraging the population to be more physically active.

This is a timely report as currently only a low number of adults, 39 per cent of men and 29 per cent of women, meet the recommendations for physical activity and these percentages are subjective or self-reported measurements. When measured objectively using accelerometery, the figures dropped to an alarmingly low 6 per cent and 4 per cent respectively (HSE 2008).

Within the past few years there has been more recognition of the role of physical activity as a support, treatment or managing factor in people with chronic disease, as evidenced by the growth of exercise referral. Sport and exercise medicine is now a recognised NHS speciality and the document 'Sport and Exercise Medicine – A Fresh Approach' (NHS 2011) outlines five key benefits of this, which are summarised in the box at the top of the next column.

Sport and exercise medicine is ideally placed to work within the NHS and private health care settings and alongside professional exercise practitioners working in exercise referral to help to promote activity adoption as a positive behaviour to help prevent, treat and manage medical conditions.

One of the barriers to 'prescribed' physical activity is the lack of access or referral to physical activity interventions, as well as barriers such as fear, lack of confidence and concerns about pain or lack of fitness. There are also concerns about a lack of resources in activity schemes that enable practitioners to address psychological and social barriers in clients together with a lack of exit routes and opportunities for clients who have completed a term of activity (NHS 2011).

1 Physical activity is a proven way of preventing expensive and debilitating diseases.

2 People suffering from chronic diseases can significantly improve their recovery and prevent co-morbidity if they exercise as part of their treatment.

3 Musculoskeletal injuries cause 50 per cent of all sickness absence in the NHS alone, at least five million days each year.

4 Getting people to exercise is a challenge, particularly unfit or ill individuals. As a result, the NHS is missing the substantial health and financial benefits associated with both prevention and treatment that exercise could bring.

5 The new speciality of Sport and Exercise Medicine (SEM) can help.

## CORRELATES OF PHYSICAL ACTIVITY

Health, sport and exercise professionals have a key role to play in encouraging people to be more active. To carry out this role effectively, it is useful for professionals to have an understanding of the factors that may impact on peoples' physical activity and sedentary behaviour.

In 2007, Bauman and Bull summarised a number of reviews carried out by researchers to identify factors that influenced physical activity. Table 2.3 summarises the Inter- and Intra-individual barriers and social correlates of physical activity in adult populations.

In reviewing some of these factors, it is clear that there are none that could be seen as direct or causal factors on physical activity (determinants), i.e. if a person has or is $X$ they will definitely be active or sedentary. Therefore, the factors listed can only be seen to be associated or correlated with

| Table 2.3 | Correlates of activity | | |
|---|---|:---:|:---:|
| **Correlates** | | **Positive** | **Negative** |
| Demographic and Biological Factors | | | |
|    Increasing Age | | | X |
|    Gender (male) | | X | |
|    Level of education | | X | |
|    Socioeconomic status | | X | |
|    Ethnicity (non-white) | | | X |
| Psychological, Cognitive and Emotional Factors | | | |
|    Perceived barriers to exercise | | | X |
|    Enjoyment of exercise | | X | |
|    Expected health benefits | | X | |
|    Intention to exercise | | X | |
|    Lack of time | | | X |
|    Perceived health or fitness | | X | |
|    Self efficacy | | X | |
|    Self-motivation | | X | |
|    Mood disturbance | | | X |
| Behavioural attributes and skills | | | |
|    Previous experience of sport and physical activity | | X | |
|    Smoking | | | X |
| Social and cultural factors | | | |
|    Social support from family | | X | |
|    Social support from friends | | X | |
| Environmental factors | | | |
|    Climate /season | | | X |
|    Access to facilities | | X | |
|    Perceived attractive neighbourhood | | X | |
|    Neighbourhood that is easy to walk around | | X | |
|    Proximity to services, shops | | X | |
| Physical activity characteristics | | | |
|    Intensity | | | X |
|    Perceived effort | | | X |
|    Leader qualities | | X | |

**Figure 2.1** Physical activity should be fun and involve social interaction

When facilitating change the practitioner, whether coach, counsellor or fitness instructor, should:

- be welcoming and friendly – have empathy with clients and create good rapport;
- be a positive role model;
- create fun sessions;
- encourage social interaction and support;
- create appropriate sessions that support increases in self-efficacy, e.g. creating opportunities for mastering new skills that are stretching but not too challenging, encouraging goal-setting and providing positive feedback;
- reward effort over performance;
- consider barriers, e.g. cost and access to facilities;
- cater for different abilities.

physical activity or sedentary behaviour (correlates). We all know active people buck the trend, but it is important that the practitioner has an understanding of potential barriers people may face when wishing to be active as it will point the way for steps the practitioner can take in developing appropriate opportunities or the right type of environment. For example, if a person does not have any support at home to be active, an exercise instructor could create a class where the members (peers) provide support for each other. Or if a sports coach is setting up a netball class for mums, they may consider the barriers that could prevent participation, for instance, childcare, and run the sessions in a facility where there is a crèche or activities are provided for children. Some examples of how an exercise instructor or sports coach could develop a supportive environment are listed below.

Further examples of specific actions the exercise instructor or sports coach can do to support behaviour change can be found in Section 3.

## SUMMARY

This chapter highlights the need for change. This includes information on the benefits of physical activity to health alongside the most recent guidelines regarding the amount and type of activity that is required to benefit health. The chapter highlights some of the correlates associated with physical activity and gives advice on how to consider these when setting up exercise and activity opportunities.

## KEY POINTS

- Despite the overwhelming evidence that physical activity benefits health, a large percentage of the population are sedentary.
- The UK Chief Medical Officers have published guidelines on the level and type of activity that people need to undertake for health.
- It is important that practitioners understand the factors (correlates) that can impact on people being active so that they can support their clients.

# THEORIES AND MODELS OF CHANGE 3

There are many different models and theories of behavioural change and each has its own central theme. In this chapter, we consider some of the key models currently in use in the field of health and physical activity together with key antecedent theories. Each of these models or theories has been simplified and discussed in the context of fitness and health, however, there is a wealth of information available on these and readers who require more in-depth information are directed to the recommended reading list at the end of the book.

## AIMS OF THIS CHAPTER:
- To outline the purpose of models and theories.
- To review key theories and models, including three-step change theory, social learning theory, social cognitive theory, self-efficacy theory, self-determination theory, the transtheoretical model of change, health action process approach, health belief model, theory of reasoned action, theory of planned behaviour.
- To review key interventions, including cognitive behavioural theory, transactional analysis, neurolinguistic programming, motivational interviewing, solution-focused/patient empowerment.
- To provide a summary of the different models, including similarities.
- To discuss person-centred adaptation of models and theories.

A person may not always choose wisely – they may make a self-destructive choice:

> Every human being has two sets of forces within him. One set clings to safety and defensiveness out of fear, tending to regress backward, hanging onto the past, afraid to grow ... afraid to take chances, afraid to jeopardise what he already has, afraid of independence, freedom, separateness. The second set of forces impels him forward toward wholeness of Self and uniqueness of Self, toward full functioning of all his capacities, toward confidence in the face of the external world at the same time that he can accept his deepest, real, unconscious Self. (Maslow, in Curzon 2004: 115)

# WHAT ARE THEORIES AND MODELS?

According to the Oxford Dictionary (Oxford University Press 2011), a theory is:

- A supposition or a system of ideas intended to explain something, especially one based on general principles independent of the thing to be explained;
- a set of principles on which the practice of an activity is based;
- an idea used to account for a situation or justify a course of action.

A model is defined as:

- A thing used as an example to follow or imitate;
- a simplified description, especially a mathematical one, of a system or process, to assist calculations and predictions.

Put simply, a theory is a hypothesis, or suggestion, of why and how behaviours develop and change, which can be tested or investigated. A model is a prediction of the factors that lead to something occurring, in this case what needs to happen or be in place or occur for behaviour change.

Change models fall very broadly into two types: staged models and psychosocial models. Each type has advantages and disadvantages and further reading is recommended to fully understand individual models and theories.

The following are common theories and models used in the field of behaviour change and while they are not the only ones, they are the most frequently encountered. It should be noted that no single model can explain how and why people change in terms of lifestyle.

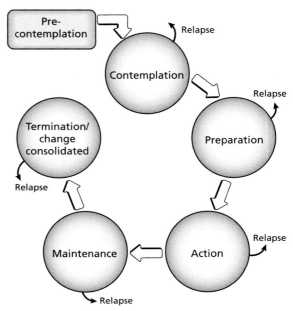

**Figure 3.1** Stages of behaviour change in the transtheoretical model

# THE TRANSTHEORETICAL MODEL OF CHANGE

Initially developed by Prochaska and DiClemente in 1983 as a tool to help with smoking and drug-use cessation, this model has become widely used in other areas of health behaviour. It utilises different stages to identify how 'ready' an individual is to make changes and suggests strategies to help 'nudge' them into a further stage.

The six stages in the transtheoretical model (TTM) are:

1   Pre-contemplation – not thinking about change
2   Contemplation – thinking about change
3   Preparation – preparing for change

4 Action – starting to change
5 Maintenance – keeping change going
6 Termination/change consolidated – the changed behaviour change is now automatic

There is a further element, relapse, represented by the anticlockwise arrows. Relapse can occur in any stage other than pre-contemplation and can undo any positive steps already made towards termination. In reality, it is rare for an individual to move through the stages in a linear fashion, people can and do move forwards and backwards through the stages many times in this model before change becomes permanent. Fava et al (1995) state that smokers may make three or four attempts at giving up before they are successful, so awareness of and preparation for lapses is important to maintain confidence in the ability to succeed. For this reason it may be more realistic to consider the TTM as a spiral model than a stepped or linear model of change.

## READINESS TO CHANGE

As with all lifestyle change, the stage of readiness to change of a person will have an impact on both the initial success and the long-term sustainability of lifestyle changes. In reality, the process is not orderly, people get stuck at certain stages and may lapse/relapse and re-enter the cycle several times before they move towards permanent changes. In 1997, Prochaska and Velicer identified that 40 per cent of at-risk populations are in pre-contemplation, 40 per cent are in contemplation, while 20 per cent are preparing to change.

The individual needs careful monitoring to ensure that appropriate strategies are employed at each stage of the process.

### Pre-contemplation

'It isn't that they can't see the solution. It is that they can't see the problem.' G.K. Chesterton may have had pre-contemplators in mind when he wrote this, as those in this stage often do not, or do not want to, acknowledge a problem. Focusing on a problem may have the effect of driving a person away from change out of fear, an informal chat ending with a suggested follow-up call in the future may be a more favourable option as it gives a person time to think – if they want to – and leaves the door open for them to return to you in the future if they decided to make a change.

### Contemplation

John is sitting in a chair, fidgeting and moaning. Jane walks past and asks what the matter is. 'This chair is really uncomfortable,' replies John. 'Why don't you move?' asks Jane. 'It's not that bad yet,' responds John.

This is typical of contemplators; they may recognise that there is a problem and may even acknowledge that they need to change, however, any discomfort or issues caused by the behaviour is not yet enough to initiate change.

At this stage, it is important to raise awareness of the benefits of change as well as discussing the negative aspects of staying the same. The aim is to move the individual from thinking about making changes to preparing to change.

### Preparation

'I'm going to start my diet/fitness programme/change on Monday/New Year's Day/next month.' Preparers fully intend to make changes 'soon' and may have already made plans for how to do it. However ready for action they appear to be, there may be some uncertainty and a need to be sure that action is the best option.

Helping to set firm goals, reinforcing the benefits of change and discussing and overcoming barriers and fears are important at this stage.

## Action

The time lapse between preparation and action is often the greatest; people may make firm plans yet not carry them through. There may be many reasons for this, including a lowering of support, as they are perceived to be 'ready' so no longer in need of nudges or guidance. In reality, the action stage is the hardest, as change is occurring and regular support should be available to keep motivation high.

Reinforce the steps already taken, highlight successes and make plans to avoid or recover from lapses to keep the individual motivated through the action stage.

## Maintenance

Once a new behaviour has been maintained for six months or more, the stage of maintenance has been reached. However, it is often wrongly assumed that once maintenance is reached, the new behaviour is firmly fixed in the individual's lifestyle.

Lapse or relapse from maintenance is likely to occur unless there is a consolidation of the new behaviour. This may mean staying away from people and places that encourage old habits or continuing to set goals and reinforce strategies for avoiding relapse.

## Termination/change consolidated

When a new behaviour is consolidated so firmly that a return to old habits is unlikely, the individual enters the final stage of termination, or change consolidated. A smoker who now considers himself or herself a *non-smoker* – rather than an *ex-smoker* or someone who is *quitting* – has reached this stage. Someone who previously overate or picked unhealthy food but now automatically chooses an overall healthy diet has also consolidated change. However, while relapse from these new habits and patterns is less likely, it is still possible, so continuing to build intrinsic motivation, reward achievement and create new goals is important for ongoing success.

This model is useful in identifying an individual's thoughts and readiness regarding changing their lifestyle. For those in pre-contemplation, it may be that an informal chat and an exchange of information is the most effective strategy, while the contemplators can be nudged into preparation with some information and a decisional balance sheet. Once an individual is in preparation, it would seem to be a small step into action, however, this is often the hardest gap to cross as there is a huge difference between wanting to change and actually changing.

Another problem with change is the likelihood of a lapse, which then becomes a relapse to previous behaviours. This may have been a pattern in the past, as the majority of obese individuals will have attempted to lose weight at least once in the past and, obviously, been unsuccessful. Their response to this 'failure' will determine their willingness to try again and their belief in their ability to succeed. The key focus of the TTM is identifying the client's readiness to change and applying appropriate interventions to move the client through the stages until maintenance, and eventually termination, is reached.

| Table 3.1 | Overview of the stages of change | | |
|---|---|---|---|
| **Stage** | **Attitude** | **Comments** | **Strategies** |
| Pre-contemplation | At the moment I'm not aware of a need to change and I have no intention of doing anything during the next six months. | This attitude may be the result of denial, fear or being overwhelmed by the problem.<br><br>Forcing someone to face the problem may result in pushing him or her further away. | Informal chat.<br><br>Highlight key benefits of the change.<br><br>Provide information leaflets.<br><br>Gather information on current lifestyle.<br><br>Arrange future appointment to reassess readiness to change. |
| Contemplation | At the moment I'm not doing anything to change but I'm thinking about doing something during the next six months. | This client is aware that a problem exists but may not be ready to address it.<br><br>Key focus here is to address ambivalence and assist towards preparation. | Discuss benefits of making the change.<br><br>Decisional balance.<br><br>Motivational interviewing.<br><br>Action planning.<br><br>SMART goal-setting. |
| Preparation | During the last year I haven't done anything to change but I'm planning to do something during the next 30 days. | This client is ready to make plans for change but may be lacking the confidence to start.<br><br>There is often a considerable time delay between preparation (intention) and action. | Reinforce benefits of making changes.<br><br>Decisional balance.<br><br>SMART goal-setting.<br><br>Action planning.<br><br>Discussion of fears surrounding change. |
| Action | I've been maintaining a change for less than six months. | By now the changed lifestyle is becoming a habit, however, it is still important to foster an internal locus of control and highlight possible lapses that may lead to relapse. | Highlight and reward success.<br><br>Reinforce benefits of changes achieved so far.<br><br>Make contingency plans. |

| Table 3.1 | Overview of the stages of change (continued) | | |
|---|---|---|---|
| Stage | Attitude | Comments | Strategies |
| Maintenance | I've kept up the change for more than six months. | Change is now a habit so developing internal coping mechanisms is key in continuing success. | Highlight and reward success. Focus on the positive benefits of change. Foster internal locus of control to manage lapses. |
| Change consolidated (termination) | I have maintained the lifestyle change for so long I can't imagine going back to the old ways. | This client now considers change normal and it is likely to be an unconscious habit. They are also likely to have a stronger internal locus of control and be able to plan for and manage lapses without relapsing. | Continue to reward success and reinforce the positive health benefits of their new behaviours. Keep making contingency plans. Consider using as a 'buddy' for newcomers. |

# THREE-STEP CHANGE THEORY

Originally developed by Kurt Lewin in 1951, this model theorises that a dynamic balance of opposing forces influences or shapes our behaviour. For example, driving forces will promote change by moving a person towards a desired behaviour, while restraining forces will prevent or block change by moving a person in the opposite direction. This means that changing a particular behaviour in the long term involves identifying these forces and using a three-step process to promote the driving balance and facilitate change.

The three steps in Lewin's model are:

1 unfreezing
2 movement or change
3 refreezing.

Let's take an ice cube as an example. It is currently a cube, however, we want it to be a sphere instead so we have two choices; we can chip away at it until it resembles a sort of sphere – but probably a smaller messy one; or we can unfreeze it, pour the water into a spherical mould and then refreeze it into the desired shape.

## UNFREEZING

Much of our behaviour is habitual, formed by experiences and includes observation and role-modelling on both conscious and unconscious levels. Habits of any kind are hard to break, so becoming ready to change will require not only the removal of existing factors that maintain the behaviour but also the addition of new motivations for changing the behaviour.

A key factor in motivation to change behaviour is acknowledging that a current behaviour is in some way negative, either in that it is causing a problem or is preventing us from moving forward. This creates the desire or need to make changes, which increases the driving force away from existing lifestyle patterns. It is important that this desire or motivation occurs to overcome the restraining forces that may obstruct changes.

There are many techniques that can be used in the unfreezing stage including:

- Visioning: This creates a motivational picture of the 'changed' state and can work well if the vision is positive and desirable.
- Goal-setting: Setting small, easy to achieve goals works well for many, however, at this stage, they should be process goals working towards the change instead of linked to change itself. For example, finding out about types of activity would be appropriate at this stage, going running would not.

## MOVEMENT

Once a behaviour pattern is identified as negative or unsatisfactory, and the motivation to change is in place, movement towards change can start.

Techniques suitable for the movement phase include:

- Boiling the frog: This involves making very small, hardly noticeable changes and is often used to facilitate changes in others – without them noticing! However, it can be adapted for use with individuals who have a history of grand attempts at change that have repeatedly failed. For example, swapping a piece of fruit for morning biscuits on three days a week is less of a 'sacrifice' than giving up biscuits altogether. (The name comes from the concept that if you throw a frog into boiling water it will simply leap back out, but if you put it in cold water and slowly increase the temperature it won't notice that it is boiling to death. Please, please don't try this at home!)
- Challenging goals: In this phase, goals can be more challenging, especially if they are linked to something that will create a sense of achievement and pride and foster the feeling of self-efficacy. For example, taking up exercise to run the Race for Life is more challenging than 'to get a bit fitter' and likely to be more motivational.
- Baby steps: making the first few phases of change easy will promote an individual's confidence in their ability to change and as each 'easy' step is achieved, the goal becomes closer.
- Change-n-chill: This technique simply involves making only one small change then allowing a period of time when the change is consolidated before making a further change. For example, trying to take up exercise, give up smoking, go on a 'diet' and stop snacking all at once is unlikely to be successful for most people as too many changes are involved. By starting with one of these, and applying some of the techniques listed above and later in the book, change is more likely to be successful and sustainable.

## REFREEZING

Once change has occurred, it needs to become established as a habit or an integral part of behaviour, hence 'refreezing'. This may also require a change in self-identity – perceiving the new behaviour as part of the self and not as 'something I'm trying to do'.

Useful techniques in this stage are based on recognising and rewarding changes made. Keeping a photographic record of weight loss or writing about achievements can help to reinforce success and help prevent sliding back into old habits. It is also important to view the behaviour as complete – for example, seeing yourself as a non-smoker rather than an ex-smoker or quitter.

## SOCIAL LEARNING THEORY

Social learning theory (SLT) evolved from behaviourism, which focused on simple stimulus-response pathways. The best known behaviourists are B. F. Skinner and Ivan Pavlov who conducted experiments in classical and operant conditioning. Albert Bandura (1977) took elements of behaviourism and added other factors that he believed were key in influencing learning.

Classical conditioning theorises that if a conditioned stimulus is put together with an unconditioned stimulus that produces an unconditioned response, this can be manipulated so that eventually the unconditioned response will occur when the conditioned stimulus alone occurs. Confused? Remember Pavlov's dogs? When the dogs saw food they started to salivate, so an association existed between food and salivation. Pavlov introduced a bell that rang as the same time as food was presented. Gradually the bell was rung earlier and earlier than the food appeared

until the dogs started to salivate purely at the sound of the bell.

An example of classical conditioning is the smell that wafts through the supermarket at certain times of year, the smell of mince pies in December is likely to, often subconsciously, trigger thoughts of Christmas and make us put more festive treats in our trolleys.

Operant conditioning suggests that the antecedent or precursor to a new behaviour pattern is based on a range of factors including the consequences of any previous behaviours. In simple terms, positive results or consequences of a previous behaviour are likely to motivate us to try a new behaviour. Operant conditioning therefore changes behaviour through positive reinforcement following the desired response. For example, a child who screams in the supermarket and is 'rewarded' with sweets to quieten them is likely to learn that the easiest way to get sweets is to throw a tantrum!

SLT suggests that there are four key factors in learning: drives, cues, responses and rewards. In 1941, Neal Miller and John Dollard hypothesised that motivation, or drive, to learn a behaviour would lead to learning via observation, which would in turn lead to imitation and finally positive reinforcement, or reward.

Bandura (1977: 22), observed: 'Learning would be exceedingly laborious, not to mention hazardous, if people had to rely solely on the effects of their own actions to inform them what to do. Fortunately, most human behaviour is learned observationally through modelling: from observing others one forms an idea of how new behaviours are performed, and on later occasions this coded information serves as a guide for action.' Using this observation – and perhaps to move away from the sometimes controversial elements of behaviourism – Bandura outlined SLT as a bridge linking behaviourist theories and later theories based on cognitive learning styles, suggesting that learning occurs within a social context, with observation, modelling and reinforcement at its centre.

There are three basic tenets underpinning SLT, which in itself differs from behaviourism in that it allows for a conscious or unconscious human element in behaviour patterns. These tenets are:

1   Response consequences: What happens when we perform acts plays a major part in determining the likelihood of behaviour being repeated. A positive consequence, such as a reward or praise, is likely to lead to repeating the behaviour, while a negative response such as anger, failure or pain may lead to giving up.

2   Vicarious learning: A form of observation, vicarious learning refers to behaviour that is learned from watching others.

3   Modelling: A key factor in observational learning, modelling suggests that humans copy behaviour seen in others. Role models can be real – friends, parents, older children – or symbolic, such as sportspeople, celebrities, leaders.

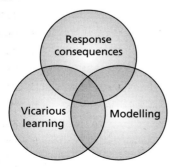

**Figure 3.2a** Factors in modelling

Modelling has four key elements:

1   Attention: Observational learning requires that attention is paid to another person's behaviour and the consequences of that behaviour. This may be by consciously watching that person or, commonly, by unconscious observation that is then stored in the mind. Additionally, observing the consequences of any behaviour or action is also important, as a perceived positive or negative consequence is likely to influence the desire to replicate the behaviour.

2   Retention: An accurate and effective mental representation of what has been observed is stored in the memory to enable replication. An inaccurate representation may lead to 'failing' to replicate the behaviour and reduce the likelihood of trying again.

3   Replication: Enacting a modelled response depends on the ability to reproduce the response by converting stored mental images into actual behaviour. There are additional considerations, for example, any 'tools' may need to be present and the ability to carry out any necessary components of that action is also important.

4   Motivation: An observed behaviour is unlikely to be reproduced unless there is motivation to do so, and motivation will depend on whether there are perceived benefits in reproducing that behaviour. If there are no perceived benefits, it is unlikely to be important enough to do so, resulting in apathy and excuses.

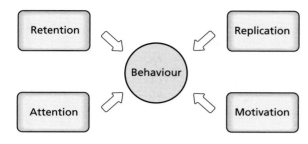

**Figure 3.2b** The three tenets of SLT

To illustrate SLT, consider how a baby learns to walk. Parents do not sit down and teach them the heel-toe action or dictate gait patterns. Babies learn from observing older children and adults walking (vicarious learning) and copying them (modelling). The usual response to the first few steps is praise and hugs (response consequences), which leads to further attempts to master this new skill. The discomfort from falling over a few times (another response consequence) is outweighed by the positive praise and encouragement received.

Throughout our lives, we meet people who have a significant impact on our behaviour development. Parents, siblings, teachers, religious leaders and friends may all affect our behaviour patterns − both consciously and unconsciously − and the earlier the influence occurs and the stronger it is, the more lasting it is likely to be.

| Table 3.2 | Role models | |
| --- | --- | --- |

Task: Consider some of the people who have influenced you during your life. Using the table below, make a note of their names, their role in your life and how they influenced you. Be honest, no one else needs to see this, so consider any negative as well as positive influences.

| Name | Role | Influence |
| --- | --- | --- |
| | | |
| | | |
| | | |
| | | |
| | | |
| | | |
| | | |
| | | |

Thus, social learning theory suggests that changing behaviour is more likely to succeed if we are around others who demonstrate the behaviour to which we aspire and if the 'rewards' of the new behaviour outweigh any discomfort from the change process.

## SOCIAL COGNITIVE THEORY

Developed by Albert Bandura (1986; 1989; 2001) from social learning theory, social cognitive theory (SCT) has three key factors; environmental, personal and behavioural.

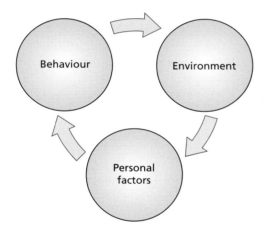

**Figure 3.3** Factors in social cognitive theory

SCT theorises that these three factors combine, although not necessarily in equal measures, to influence the outcome expectation of a behaviour or a change in behaviour. These form a 'reality' that may dictate whether the individual believes change is 'possible' for them, they may see themselves as unable to change or be unable to visualise themselves in the changed state, which

will affect their willingness to attempt change as their inner reality says that 'I can't do this'.

The role of the environment in which we live or work also plays a part in learned behaviour and changing behaviour as both our physical and social environment influence our choices and decisions.

Consider the two pictures below; what might a person feel if they live in one of these environments? How might their surroundings impact on their quality of life or behaviour patterns?

Now think about an environment in which you have felt secure or insecure, safe or unsafe, comfortable or out of place. How did you behave as a result?

**Figure 3.4a** Country village

**Figure 3.4b** City

| Table 3.3 | Environmental influences | |
|-----------|--------------------------|---|
| **Place** | **How it made you feel** | **How you behaved** |
| | | |
| | | |
| | | |
| | | |
| | | |

Personal factors, or our inner 'self', also shape our behaviour. This sense of self is a complex mix of previous experiences, perceptions, ability and confidence and feelings about previous success or failure. These form a subconscious 'truth' about our self, which has a strong effect on our conscious confidence or willingness to attempt a change in behaviour.

This inner reality or self-efficacy is fundamental to SCT – as the interaction between our behaviour, personal thoughts or beliefs and our environment often dictates our sense of who we are and what we are capable of doing. Phrases such as those below are indications of an inner reality that may be the result of this interaction rather than from actual experiences.

- 'My family have always been ...'
- 'I'm not that type ...'
- 'People like me don't ...'

This sense of who we are can be a powerful motivation, or an equally strong barrier to change, so any goal or outcome must match the internal 'truths' of a person and those truths must include a sense of being able to overcome barriers.

If we believe we can't achieve something, a vicious cycle of failed attempts is likely to lead to low self-efficacy, while believing that we can is likely to result in a virtuous cycle of success.

## SELF-EFFICACY THEORY

Self-efficacy theory evolves further from SCT and the work of Albert Bandura (1977), whose studies focused on how thinking processes may influence behaviour change (cognitive behaviour modification).

Self-efficacy focuses on an individual's *perceived confidence* regarding their ability to perform a specific action, behaviour or task, for example:

- Confidence to start an exercise programme.
- Confidence to stop smoking.
- Confidence to attend a study group.
- Confidence to perform a cartwheel.

> 'Whether you think you can, whether you think you cannot, you are 100% correct!'
> Henry Ford

Bandura believed that an individual's perception of their ability was a key factor determining their motivation:

- To initiate a change (intention).
- To expend effort making the change (volition).
- To persist and keep going (adherence).

For example: An individual who perceived they *were* able to do something (change a behaviour or perform a task) would be more inclined to take on the challenge and keep it going, whereas an individual who *did not* believe they could do something would be less likely to start the task and if they did, would be less to keep it going (relapse).

Bandura also believed that there were two key aspects of efficacy that would influence confidence in exercise and physical activity:

1   Efficacy expectations: An individual's beliefs about their own self-competence
2   Outcome expectations: An individual's beliefs regarding the perceived result or outcome of doing something. For example, if a person believes that something will not work, then it is likely that it will not.

Bandura (1977) identified four primary sources that inform self-efficacy:

1   Performance attainment: Possibly the most powerful of the four, because it is based on personal experience of success or failure. Success increases efficacy, whereas failure reduces. Failure may be linked to previous negative experiences, especially those that are attached to a negative emotion being evoked, such as humiliation or shame. For example, coming last in a race at school, being the one always picked last for a team or being consciously aware that you are the only one in an exercise class who is not able to keep up.

2   Imitation and modelling: Seeing others who are very similar to yourself succeed or fail can enhance own self-efficacy if you have no prior experience. For example, seeing a person with the same condition taking part in exercise or completing a marathon can create the feeling 'if they can do it, so can I'. Alternatively, having a role model (an elite athlete or sporting star) can provide a motivational goal – 'I want to be like that'.

3   Verbal and social persuasion: Being influenced by another person to do something. This may be effective if the person's opinion is respected and valued.

4   Judgements of physical states: How the person interprets a physiological response. This is of particular relevance for people with mental health conditions, as many of the initial physiological effects of exercise (increased heart rate, sweating, increased breathlessness, etc.) are the same as the side effects of some medication and the same as the symptoms of some mental conditions (e.g. panic attacks, etc.).

Sport and exercise professionals can help clients improve their self-efficacy by using the following restructuring strategies that can help an individual to reframe and restructure their thinking processes (cognitions) in relation to exercise and physical activity:

- Providing education regarding the immediate effects of exercise (e.g. you will start to feel warm and your heart rate may increase and you may begin to perspire, etc.) may help an individual to recognise their body's response to the exercise, rather than a symptom of a condition or medication.
- Providing a positive environment, where individuals are valued and supported (core conditions).
- Offering adaptations and alternatives to promote inclusion, rather than creating exclusion.
- Offering praise, especially to newcomers who may need assistance with building their confidence.
- Promoting exercise as a reward, rather than a punishment! For example, encouraging exercise as a daily reward for the self (taking care of the self), rather than promoting it as a compensatory behaviour for eating too much (a punishment).
- Promoting self-monitoring rather than competition.
- Promoting the use of positive self-talk that the person can use to assist their efficacy and motivation before and during exercise.
- Providing resources (handouts, fact sheets) that give information of the positive effects of exercise.
- Promoting the rewards of exercise (health and other benefits).

- Being mindful of the individual's physiological response that occurs when they think about exercising. This may be out of their conscious awareness, but has the potential to be a large barrier to participation. For example, if an individual inwardly groans at the thought of exercise and perceives exercise as hard work or a punishment, then this cognition will need to be reframed.

## SELF-DETERMINATION THEORY

Self-determination theory (SDT) offers a broad framework for the study of motivation and personality. SDT evolves from the work of Richard Ryan and Edward Deci (1995) who suggest that people can either be *proactive and engaged* or *passive and alienated* (motivated or amotivated) and that their level of motivation is largely in response to the *social conditions* in which they develop and function.

Self-determination theory focuses on the interrelationship between *intrinsic* and *extrinsic motivation* and the *innate needs* for: competence, autonomy, and social relatedness, which they believe are key psychological needs for intrinsically motivated behaviour. It is suggested that motivation can be enhanced by creating environments that support an individual's experience of competence, autonomy and relatedness (see definitions below) and will foster the strongest forms of motivation (Biddle and Mutrie 2001: 80). Alternatively, in environments where these innate needs are not supported, motivation will be reduced.

- Competence: Being in control of outcomes, being successful, experiencing mastery (e.g. recognising personal power and ability to have control in events, will increase motivation).
- Autonomy: Being one's own 'self-determined' authority and master of own destiny (e.g. having a choice and being able to make own decisions and doing something because you want to, rather than because you ought to or have to).

High levels of autonomy and choice will foster higher levels of motivation. In addition, the more internalised any extrinsic motivational factors are (see Figure 3.5), the more autonomous the person.

- Relatedness: Being connected to others, relating to others. The more supportive the environment, the more positive the impact on self-determined motivation.

| Level of self determination | Source of motivation | Example statement |
|---|---|---|
| No motivation | Amotivation<br>There is little or no motivation<br>The value of doing something is not seen | I can't be bothered to exercise |
| Threshold of motivation<br>Low motivation | Extrinsic<br><br>External regulation<br>Action is motivated by rewards or threats from others<br>e.g. exercise on prescription | I will exercise if I must or I am exercising because my GP told me I should |
| | Introjected regulation<br>Action is motivated by the need for approval from others or to avoid negative feelings<br>When the value of something is taken in but not seen as one's own | I feel guilty if I don't exercise<br>I exercise because I have to or ought to |
| Threshold for autonomy | Identified regulation<br>Action is motivated by an appreciation of the outcomes | I want to exercise, it is important to me |
| The most self-determined form of extrinsic motivation<br>High motivation | Integrated regulation<br>Action is motivated to achieve personal goals<br><br>Intrinsic motivation<br>Action is motivated by pleasure | I exercise because it is my choice, it is part of who I am<br>I exercise because it is fun and I enjoy it |
| For its own sake | | |

**Figure 3.5** Continuum of motivation (adapted from Biddle and Mutrie 2001: 86)

# HEALTH ACTION PROCESS APPROACH

The Health Action Process Approach (HAPA) was developed by Ralf Schwarzer, Professor of Psychology at the Freie University of Berlin, Germany, and is a *hybrid* model that integrates aspects from both motivational and behavioural-enabling models (Biddle and Mutrie 2001: 69).

The approach suggests that changing behaviour is a process that consists of two main phases:

1   The motivation phase: Setting the intention to make a change and potentially following this through to planning (links with TTM contemplation and planning stages).
2   The volition phase: Following the intention through to action (links with TTM action and maintenance stages).

Successful transition from the motivation phase to the volition phase will demand a shift and change in mindset (Biddle and Mutrie 2001). In cognitive behavioural therapy (CBT) terms, the individual will need to reframe their thoughts (cognitions) to enable this transition.

Success at each stage and throughout the process can be predicted by three main factors:

1   The individual's *self-efficacy*;
2   Their *outcome expectancy*;
3   Perceived risks or *risk perception*.

Self-efficacy: The more a person believes they are capable of making a change, the higher the likelihood for success. Any self-doubt and lack of self-belief will make it less likely that a change will be initiated.

Outcome expectancies: If the person anticipates a successful outcome, they are more likely to follow through with action. If they anticipate failure, they are unlikely to follow through. For example, a person who has tried to give up smoking in the past and relapsed may well find that their self-talk and perceived efficacy diffuses the formation of any further positive intentions, despite the attractiveness of the expected outcome. See also cognitive dissonance on page 52.

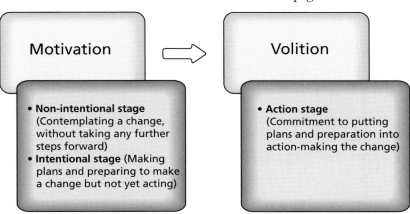

**Figure 3.6** Motivation and volition stages

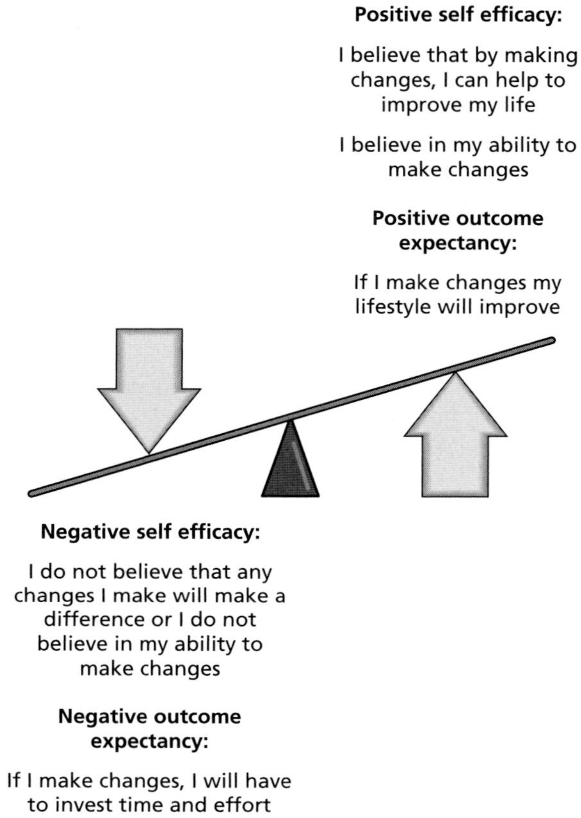

**Positive self efficacy:**

I believe that by making changes, I can help to improve my life

I believe in my ability to make changes

**Positive outcome expectancy:**

If I make changes my lifestyle will improve

**Negative self efficacy:**

I do not believe that any changes I make will make a difference or I do not believe in my ability to make changes

**Negative outcome expectancy:**

If I make changes, I will have to invest time and effort

**Figure 3.7** Positive vs. negative self-efficacy

Ultimately, the more positive the self-belief, and the more positive the anticipated outcome, the higher will be the likelihood to put the intention into action.

Risk perceptions: Awareness of the risks attached with specific behaviour (e.g. the risk of inactivity, smoking) often pushes the individual into contemplation. While a minimum level of threat needs to be recognised before any change is contemplated, appealing to fear holds limited value. There have been numerous campaigns to promote health, appealing to fear of consequences for maintaining specific behaviours (coronary heart disease and smoking, alcohol, diet, inactivity, etc.), yet the problem behaviours continue to persist. Thus, self-efficacy and outcome expectancies potentially play a stronger role in moving the mindset forward from motivation to volition.

Encouraging change: Any persuasive techniques for promoting change (moving the individual from motivation to volition) should be framed in a way that allows individuals to identify and draw on their coping resources and potential skills. Every person has an abundance of these skills and resources; the key is to facilitate and enable the person to find them and use them.

Promoting self-efficacy: Instead of emphasising, enlarging and playing on fear (of failure and not being able to make a change), the emphasis of persuasion should be placed on the individual's potential competence, their skills to cope and manage. This technique promotes minimisation of fear and reframes this as something the person can manage and handle (building self-efficacy rather than diminishing it).

Challenging ambivalence: When weighing up the risks associated with their current behaviour and the desire to make changes, an individual may find they experience some inner resistance (ambivalence). Part of them will want to change and will be able to list all the reasons for changing their behaviour; another part of them may not want to change and will be able to list numerous reasons for not changing their behaviour. In motivational interviewing, discussed later, this is referred to as change talk and sustain talk. The individual should be encouraged to speak from their change talk position rather than their sustain talk position, to increase their motivation to move forward towards volition.

Goal-setting: Once an intention has been shaped in the motivation phase, this has to be framed as a detailed set of instructions that provide a guide to how to get there. For example, a person with the intention to be more active will need specific guidance on how often they need to be active, for how long, what type of activities, what to wear, how this will develop over time, etc. They need advice, guidance and different options for how they may achieve their goal.

Small steps or giant leaps: The volitional phase is influenced mainly by self-efficacy, which determines both the effort the person will put in and their perseverance to sustain the change. In practice, an individual with a higher self-efficacy (competence and experience) may have a higher number of and higher quality (more challenging) action plans (bigger steps to making the change). An individual with lower self-efficacy would be encouraged to work towards smaller targets and with fewer action plans initially, with the aim being to build their efficacy – a 'one step at a time approach' to making changes.

Visualisation: Individuals with a lower self-efficacy may anticipate failure and doubt their ability to handle situations, which may contribute to them prematurely aborting their attempt to make changes. Alternatively, those with a higher and more positive self-efficacy are more likely to visualise success and find ways of coping and persevering when obstacles arise.

Individuals can be encouraged to use visualisation techniques (that support their change) more regularly, so that they begin to develop the sight of seeing themselves as they would like to be.

Relapse: In any change situation, there is potential for relapse and returning to old behaviours. An individual with a higher self-efficacy is likely to be more able to recover from relapse scenarios more effectively because they are more able to regain self-control and survive the critical situation.

Individuals will usually require some help to identify triggers and high risk situations and will need to explore ways of managing these situations, by either reframing their thoughts (how to manage their thoughts when in a high-risk situation or when a behaviour is triggered) and/or using avoidance behaviour (not exposing self to the risk situation). The more aware the individual is of their thinking in these high-risk situations, the easier it will be for them to manage their urges and behaviour. For example, an individual who finds themselves feeling stressed and reaching for a cigarette when stuck in traffic, can train their mind to respond in a different way in these situations. They can prepare for the experience of being in the situation and put strategies in place. Similarly, someone who has already experienced the high-risk situation and coped previously will be aware that they have the strategies to manage the situation.

Relapse itself can also be reframed, so that it is seen not as a failure but as an opportunity to learn something about oneself.

## Table 3.4    Stages and interventions

| Motivation phase | Volition phase | Self-determination phase |
|---|---|---|
| Build intention | Build coping skills and promote self-efficacy. | Promote recovery/relapse. |
| Building the pathways to establishing the intention to change. | Set goals and prepare for setbacks. | Maintaining self-efficacy and promote re-engagement in the event of relapse. |
| Build self-efficacy. | Use action planning steps appropriate to the efficacy of the individual, some people will need smaller steps and a slower approach and others may take larger leaps and make changes at a faster pace. | Recognise risks and triggers. |
| Provide information handouts to identify benefits of making a change (focus on benefits for changing rather than risks of not changing). | | Prepare strategies in the event of relapse: |
| Highlight the individual's resources (inner and outer). | | Respond; Initiate re-engagement; Maintenance; Recovery. |
| Promote their competence and skills. | | |
| Promote change talk, rather than sustain talk. | | |
| Outcome expectancy. | Coping strategy planning. | Barriers and resources. |
| Promote focus on the desired outcome. | Offer tools to manage relapse to setbacks. | Be aware of high risk and trigger situations and avoid these if necessary to reduce cravings or temptation. |
| Visualise success. | | Find resources to overcome all perceived barriers and obstacles or blocks to success. |
| Reframe thoughts regarding failure (no one fails). | | Find outer supporters e.g. people who will encourage and support the person through their change (secure social support). |
| Risk perception. | Positive mental attitude. | Disengagement or engagement. |
| Promote belief in their competence and ability to handle situations. | Build the 'I can handle it' mentality. | Reframe lapse and relapse as part of the journey, these experiences allow lessons to be learned and the potential for new coping strategies to be put into place. |

# THE HEALTH BELIEF MODEL

One of the most enduring theories of health behaviour, the health belief model (Rosenstock 1966) suggests that beliefs and perceptions need to be clear to encourage an individual to take steps to change their behaviour in order to benefit or protect their health.

Change is most likely to occur if the individual believes that:

- They are susceptible to or at risk of a problem.
- The perceived consequences of that problem cause concern to them.
- The necessary action will provide benefits.
- Any barriers are outweighed by the benefits.

The key message from the health belief model is that the client needs to be aware of and be concerned about any risk or consequences of a behaviour and believe that the benefits gained from changing that behaviour outweigh the barriers that must be overcome.

# THEORY OF REASONED ACTION

This theory, initially developed by Martin Fishbein and Icek Ajzen (1975; 1980) suggests that the consequences of a behaviour are considered prior to performing it. These perceived consequences may come from the individual's thoughts or from societal pressures and change is more likely to occur if both are congruent.

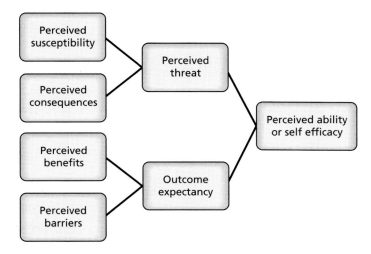

**Figure 3.8** The health belief model

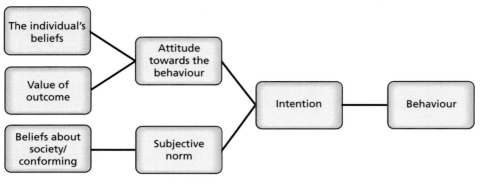

**Figure 3.9** The theory of reasoned action model

## THEORY OF PLANNED BEHAVIOUR

Expanding on the theory of reasoned action, Ajzen (1985) developed the theory of planned behaviour, which adds in factors to the intention of change that are outside the control of the individual. The amount of control an individual has over planned changes will determine the successful outcome. Ajzen suggests that self-efficacy and the sense of control an individual perceives they have are both important factors in the strength of the intention to perform behaviours and the actual behaviour.

The key elements of these two models are outlined below:

• Attitude to behaviour: This is determined by a belief in a desired or valued outcome from adopting or continuing a particular behaviour

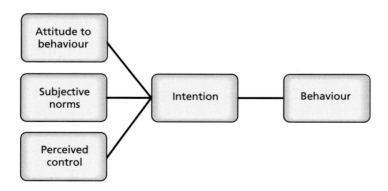

**Figure 3.10** The theory of planned behaviour

- Subjective norms: The subjective norm is an individual's perceptions of both what they believe and what society or peers think or believe, for example, if someone lives in a country where the perception is that certain sports are a bit feminine this may affect participation
- Perceived control: Behaviour is more likely to be adopted or changed if the individual believes they have control over their ability to do so.

The combination of these three elements forms the intention, from which behaviour change is likely to follow.

## I-CHANGE MODEL

A stepped model, I-Change has its roots in a range of theories including social cognitive theory, theory of planned behaviour, the transtheoretical model, the health belief model and goal-setting.

There are three phases of change, awareness, motivation and action.

Awareness is a combination of knowledge and information combined with risk perception relating to a particular behaviour. This must be an accurate assessment of knowledge and perception, for example, a person who knows the recommended physical activity guidelines and believes they are meeting them is unlikely to perceive a lack of activity to be a factor in their risk of disease. However, using a tool such as a pedometer or accelerometer or a discussion with a professional may cause them to rethink their activity levels and become aware of the risks associated with inactivity.

To change a behaviour requires motivation and this is dependent on the person's internal beliefs (perceived risk and benefits), the value they place on the outcome (outcome expectancy) and their belief in their ability to make the change (self-efficacy).

The step from motivation to action is not necessarily simple or immediate. Wanting to change may not lead to changing and while awareness and motivation may be high, making a definite plan and making a change may take time. Self-efficacy is key in action combined with goal-setting and action planning, for progress as well as relapse.

## LOCUS OF CONTROL THEORY

An individual's locus of control is a major competence motive. It is the extent to which an individual believes they are in control of their own destiny (Gross 1996: 113) and is a learned behaviour, in that if an individual's freedom (their perceived control) is threatened, then their reaction will be to reassert their control (psychological reactance) and take some form of action. However, if loss of control is repeatedly experienced, the individual may develop a 'learned helplessness' (Seligman 1975, in Gross 1996: 117). That is, they learn to believe that anything they do will not make a difference, and may develop a more externally driven locus of control.

When working with individuals, it is helpful to recognise whether they have stronger internal or external locus of control. An individual with a higher external locus of control will need more guidance and support through the process of making changes, so that they are able to recognise the extent to which they do have power and are able to have some control. They will need more encouragement and motivation through the process to relearn their own competence.

| Table 3.5 | Locus of control theory | |
|---|---|---|
| | **Internal locus of control** | **External locus of control** |
| Level of responsibility | Believe they have control of what happens in their lives – takes ownership. Masters of their own destiny (e.g. if diagnosed with a health condition, they are more likely to gather information and explore potential changes they can make). | Believes external factors (other people, luck, fate) control their lives. Fatalistic (e.g. if diagnosed with a health condition, they will need to be guided and supported towards exploring sources for gathering information and possible changes. They may need more direction, short-term goal-setting and signposting). |
| Motivation and self-determination | Higher levels of self-motivation. When they have made their mind up to do something (commitment), they usually follow through with action and stick with it (adherence) – more likely to find ways to be active, take part in unsupervised exercise. | Any perceived risk of failure, will decrease their likelihood to commit to making a change (learned helplessness). When they do engage with making a change, they may quickly lose belief and motivation and may either modify the original goal or give up altogether – more likely to need ongoing support and guidance and progress checks, will need supervised exercise. |
| Rewards | Need less external rewards, encouragement and support. | Need more external rewards, encouragement and support. |
| Peer pressure | Less likely to succumb to peer pressure. | More likely to succumb to peer pressure and give in or give up. |

# COGNITIVE DISSONANCE

Cognitive dissonance theory evolves from the work of Leon Festinger (1957, in Leith. 1994: 13 and Gross 1996: 448) Cognitive dissonance is the state of inner conflict and discomfort that occurs when an individual holds two or more conflicting beliefs, which are contradictory to each other.

## EXAMPLE 1

If an individual smokes, but also knows that smoking causes chronic diseases (coronary heart disease, chronic obstructive pulmonary disease, cancer, etc.), they have two conflicting cognitions:

(1) 'They smoke'; and (2) 'Smoking causes health problems' (Gross 1996: 448). Their behaviour is incongruent with their belief.

To resolve the dissonance, the individual needs to either change the behaviour or change their attitude towards the behaviour and there are many ways of doing this. The healthiest option is to give up smoking (change the behaviour). The unhealthy options include a range of methods by which they can change their attitude about the behaviour, for example: dismissing the evidence base that links smoking with chronic conditions (not all smokers get cancer), or smoking low tar cigarettes (in an attempt to reduce the risk); convincing themselves that smoking brings pleasure and reduces uncomfortable stress or helps to prevent them gaining weight; or associating with others who smoke (e.g. I have seen nurses smoke, so it cannot be dangerous); flaunting the danger and continuing to smoke anyway (Gross 1996: 448).

## EXAMPLE 2

An individual who exercises regularly, despite knowing that exercise can sometimes be uncomfortable – it demands effort and exertion, you get breathless, hot and sweaty, muscles start working and aching, etc. – has to find a way of overcoming the negative reaction to justify their continuation of the behaviour (Leith 1994: 13).

Leith suggests that to overcome the dissonance the individual has to remind themselves mentally that exercise is good for them, that they will feel better after, etc. This is one theory reported to explain the shift in attitude and mood towards a more positive state after exercise, and which enhances mental well-being.

## DISSONANCE AND DECISION-MAKING

When making a choice between two equally appealing options (e.g. when buying a new car), individuals will have to emphasise the undesirable qualities of the option they reject and avoid information which emphasises its desirable qualities (see Figure 3.11).

In relation to an unhealthy behaviour, an individual would need to raise the profile and highlight the benefits (for them) of the unhealthy behaviour and underemphasise the positive benefits (for them) and, in addition, avoid any

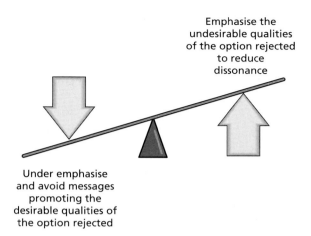

Emphasise the undesirable qualities of the option rejected to reduce dissonance

Under emphasise and avoid messages promoting the desirable qualities of the option rejected

**Figure 3.11** Dissonance and decision-making

messages promoting the alternative behaviour as this would serve to recreate the dissonance (raising anxiety and fear)

## DISSONANCE, ATTITUDES, BEHAVIOURS AND CHOICE

Dissonance only occurs with *volitional behaviour*, that is behaviour that is an action of our own free will. It does not occur when an individual believes they have no choice. The power of choice therefore potentially offers a double-edged sword – to choose wisely or not wisely. There are a number of ways individuals can rationalise (find reasons to support and defend) their choices and dissonance theory regards the human being not as a rational creature but a *rationalising* one, attempting to appear 'rational' both to themselves and others (Gross 1996: 449).

In practice, these conflicting beliefs can be worked with and explored. The helper can use motivational interviewing techniques to identify 'change talk' and 'sustain talk' (reasons for changing and reasons for not changing a behaviour). The decisional balance sheet can also be used. The aim of the intervention should be to encourage the person to speak more often and more positively from 'the change' position as this may help to move them towards actually making a change.

## SUMMARY

In reviewing the models presented it must be recalled that many of them were developed to help describe other health behaviours and were not directly developed for understanding participation in physical activity.

> Models established in other areas of health behaviour may not apply … exercise is a positive behaviour which people have to start and continue rather than (as with most health behaviours) a negative behaviour which has to be stopped. (Donaghy and Mutrie 1999: 77)

In 2007, the National Institute of Health and Clinical Excellence (NICE) conducted a review of behaviour change and physical activity and indicated that they could not find evidence to specifically recommend one specific model but suggested that practitioners should employ a range of behaviour change methods and approaches and develop interventions that take account of social, environmental and economic contexts.

So what elements from these models should practitioners focus on to ensure that they are effective in creating long term adherence in physical activity?

1  Personal and environmental factors – the practitioner needs to have an understanding of the barriers and supporting factors that are associated with physical activity (see section on correlates). A number of the models highlight the importance of a client having weighed up the risks and benefits of physical activity before becoming ready to change; practitioners should be aware of tools and techniques, such as decisional balance and encouraging change talk, to support clients in tipping the balance.

2  Self-efficacy – this is consistently associated with physical activity. Practitioners need to be clear how they can increase and maintain the self-efficacy of their clients. It needs to be remembered that self-efficacy can change depending upon the activity being undertaken. For example, a client may be comfortable in their ability to undertake a walking programme but is likely to be less comfortable if asked to undertake a ski jump!

3  Support – people are influenced by the perceived support that they have around them and whether being active is seen as appropriate by their peers. It is important that the practitioner takes this into consideration and creates a supportive environment for the client.

4  Motivation – practitioners need to have a good understanding of theories that focus on increasing and maintaining motivation over time, in particular the difference between intrinsic and extrinsic motivation. It is important to consider both the role of motivation in taking up physical activity but also its role in maintaining activity over time.

5  Stage or phase of behaviour change – the practitioner needs to consider what stage the client is at and be aware of correct techniques to apply at each stage to support clients to move on to action alongside how to prevent and/or deal with clients who may have relapsed.

Sections 2 and 3 will provide detail on tools and techniques that practitioners can use to address these elements.

# INTERVENTIONS

There are a range of change interventions and/or models of working with clients that have been developed to support the models and theories. These include techniques such as cognitive behavioural therapy, neurolinguistic programming, transactional analysis, motivational interviewing, solution-focused interventions and managing lapses.

## COGNITIVE BEHAVIOURAL THERAPY

Cognitive behavioural therapy (CBT) is one of the most widely used talking therapies in the UK. It is the model of talking therapy that is most favoured by the NHS and NICE and is recommended as part of the treatment plan of a range of mental health conditions, including depression, anxiety disorders and bulimia nervosa.

CBT shares theories from both behavioural theory (learned and conditioned responses) and cognitive theory (our thoughts and belief systems impact how we feel and behave). It evolves from the work of Albert Ellis, who developed rational emotive therapy (rational emotive counselling), and Aaron Beck, whose approach is the most evidence-based and widely used.

Key themes of the cognitive model include: irrational beliefs and the ABC model (Ellis), automatic/negative automatic thoughts (NATs) and schemas (Beck).

### Irrational beliefs

Ellis identified a number of irrational beliefs that he believed contributed to human suffering. One example is: 'I must be good at everything and at all times. Otherwise I am not a worthwhile person.' The irrationality in this belief is that nobody can be good at all things all the time. Trying to live up to this belief would cause an individual incredible stress, would lead to competitiveness and may contribute towards striving for conventional achievement and success, while neglecting own 'self' values.

### ABC model (activating event, beliefs and consequence)

Ellis believed how people think about situations is one of the greatest contributory factors to how they feel. Much of human thinking is irrational and the cause of their unhappiness. Ellis believed that if thinking patterns are reframed then experiences will be less devastating.

| Table 3.6 | ABC model | |
|---|---|---|
| **Activating event** | **Beliefs and inference** | **Emotional and behavioural consequence** |
| Failing an exam or test | Irrational:<br>It is awful to fail<br>I am a failure, I am useless | Depressed, hopeless<br>Gives up |
| *Alternative response* | | |
| Failing an exam or test | Rational:<br>It is disappointing to fail<br>Never mind, I will study some more | Feels disappointed and irritated<br>Will take the test again |

## Automatic thoughts

Beck suggested that most cognitions and thoughts are automatic. They are usually on the edge of person's awareness and form part of their inner dialogue (how they speak to themselves). He used the term negative automatic thoughts (NATs).

## Schemas

Schemas are the templates people use to filter incoming information, which define the underlying beliefs they hold about themselves, others and the world and which are usually learned through early childhood experiences and social learning or modelling from others, e.g. parents (Feltham and Horton 2000: 316).

Beck believed that most psychological disturbances are caused by the way people process their experiences and by dysfunctional thinking. He believed that maladaptive schemas were negative, rigid and absolute and when activated would influence all aspects of information processing (Feltham and Horton 2000: 316). Thus, any schema (thoughts and beliefs) an individual held about themselves would be used to distort any other incoming information, causing dysfunctional processing, for example:

- Drawing conclusions without supporting evidence (arbitrary inference).
- Thinking dichotomously – thinking in extremes; things are marvellous or terrible, there is no middle ground.
- Maximising or minimising – making things more important or less important than they actually are, e.g. a normally considerate and compassionate person losing their temper and drawing the conclusion that they are a bad person.

CBT offers a structured, goal-orientated and problem-solving approach to change and the primary focus of the work is on thinking patterns (cognitions). The main goal is to eradicate irrational beliefs and develop healthier, more functional thinking patterns using techniques that are logical, directive, persuasive and re-educative (Hough 1994: 101).

The focus of CBT work is on the present and the future. The past may be considered, but deep insight and understanding of what has gone before is not the focus. Some of the theoretical concepts emphasised by other models are not prioritised in CBT. For example:

- Empathy (person-centred) is not stressed as a priority and the helper is encouraged to stay more detached and not become enmeshed in the client's irrational thinking.
- Transference (psychodynamic) would not be evoked; although it may be openly discussed to challenge any irrational beliefs of needing to be loved and accepted by all people all of the time (Hough 1994: 100).
- Non-directive working (person-centred) is not advocated. Ellis believed that people who were emotionally disturbed needed to be authoritatively taught to accept themselves and others (directed).

Some of the techniques used in CBT may include:

- Education, e.g. raising the person's awareness to different thinking patterns, teaching them to reality test any distortions of their own thinking, and helping the individual to understand the effects of thoughts on behaviours, feelings and physiology.

- The use of homework, e.g. keeping a diary to monitor thinking patterns or practising assertive communication in situations where they may be unassertive.
- Bibliotherapy, e.g. the recommendation of reading (self-help books, etc.) to gain more information.
- Role play, e.g. rehearsing how they may act and behave in a situation.
- Relaxation, e.g. using relaxation techniques to reduce anxiety and provide a coping strategy in times of stress.
- Scheduling activities, e.g. to increase activity levels, specific activities are scheduled into the day.
- Positive reinforcement, e.g. positively reinforcing the desired behaviour.

## NEUROLINGUISTIC PROGRAMMING

Human beings' behaviour, no matter how bizarre it may first appear to be, makes sense when it is seen in the context of the choices generated by their 'model' (how they see the world). The difficulty is not that they are making the wrong choice but that they do not have enough choices – they don't have a richly focused image of the world. (Bandler and Grinder 1975: 14)

Neurolinguistic programming (NLP) has its origins in the early 1970s when Dr Richard Bandler and Dr John Grinder, who were based at the University of California, studied and modelled three successful therapists and integrated their findings with research from psychology and linguistics. As the name suggests, the focus of NLP is the use of language, and how people use words to inform themselves and others. NLP practitioners believe that this use of language can influence peoples' perception of reality and therefore their behaviour.

NLP uses a client-centred approach and includes a number of tools and techniques that can help support behaviour change, for example, in building rapport, setting and visualisation of goals, and modelling of behaviour. NLP practitioners believe that all behaviour or habits start with the brain and thought, and if we can choose where to focus our attention and take control of the conscious mind, we will build up new patterns of thinking that influence new behaviours. A key aim of NLP is to help clients develop more choice and control in their lives. Examples of NLP techniques that support behaviour change have been included in Section 3.

## TRANSACTIONAL ANALYSIS

You cannot teach a man anything. You can only help him discover it within himself. (Galileo, in James and Jongeward 1996: 1)

Transactional analysis (TA) is variously described as: 'a theory of personality'; 'a systematic psychotherapy for personal growth and change'; a theory of communication; and a model for understanding childhood development (Stewart and Joines 1987: 3). TA evolves from the work of Eric Berne and offers some potentially valuable insights into concepts that may block an individual's personal growth and the change process where there is 'a need for understanding of individuals, relationships and communication' (Stewart and Joines 1987: 3). It is complex, however, so only a very brief and basic introduction and overview can be provided here. Those interested in exploring the model further are referred to some texts referenced throughout subsequent paragraphs, which are fully listed in the references.

Briefly, some of the key themes and concepts for understanding how the TA model operates include:

- Ego states – parent/adult/child (PAC)
- Transactions and strokes
- The OK philosophy
- Life scripts
- Life positions
- Games and rackets
- The drama triangle and roles (Victim, Persecutor, Rescuer)
- Autonomy and power triangle.

## Ego states – parent/adult/child

One key theme of the TA model is the concept that people operate from different ego states when they communicate, that is, the behaviour, thinking and feeling they are displaying at the specific time, originates from a different aspect of the personality; namely the parent, adult or child ego states.

These ego states may reflect internal communication (how we communicate with ourselves – our inner self-talk and dialogue) and external communication (how we communicate with others and how others communicate with us).

The behaviours, thoughts and feelings we display are only classed as representing an ego state, when they consistently occur together in specific situations (Stewart and Joines 1987: 15). They are not right or wrong, they are just different

| **Parent**<br>Responding in a way that mirrors thoughts, feelings and behaviours displayed by a parent, parental figure or primary caregiver | • Critical Parent (the inner bully), which attacks self esteem, e.g. 'That was a stupid thing to do', 'You will never amount to much'<br>• Nurturing Parent (the inner carer), which builds self esteem, e.g Make sure you wear that nice warm jumper', 'Well done!' |
|---|---|
| **Adult**<br>Responding using own thinking, feeling and behaviour in the here and now, like a grown-up | • Asking for something you want, e.g. 'What's the time?'<br>• Explaining your thoughts and feelings to someone assertively<br>• Acting reasonably in spite of feelings (e.g. depressed, sulky, aggressive, etc.) |
| **Child**<br>Responding in a way that resembles behaviours, thoughts and feelings that one used as a child | • Adapted Child – behaving in a specific way to please others (saying please and thank you)<br>• Rebellious Child – behaving in a way that opposes others (sulking if we don't get our own way)<br>• Free Child – e.g. if someone pushes you, pushing them back or risk taking behaviours |

**Figure 3.12** Ego states

and can contribute to different outcomes from communication and experiences (whether we feel good or bad). For example, when someone makes a mistake, they may internally berate themselves (critical parent/persecuting) and end up feeling bad. They may deny any responsibility – 'It wasn't my fault' – (child), may feel helpless or like a victim, or may choose to recognise that sometimes mistakes are made and learn from the experience and seek to correct it (adult).

One aim of TA is to move any consistent communication patterns (internal and external dialogue) into consciousness as these patterns can be changed to achieve more positive outcomes in many areas of life.

## The OK philosophy

The underpinning philosophy of the TA model is that in essence all people are OK – they have worth, dignity and value and are equal (I'm OK, you're OK), there is no judgement that puts any person as one up or one down from another. Furthermore, people also have the capacity to think, and take responsibility for their choices and decisions, which includes living with the consequences of these decisions, and making changes to these decisions if they so desire.

A working contract in TA therapy would reflect the equality of responsibility. The client would express what they want and what they are willing to do to bring about the desired change and the helper would agree to work with them (Stewart and Joines 1987: 8).

## Life scripts

TA theory suggests that in early childhood people sketch out a life script that outlines how their life will operate and includes the life position they adopt (OK or Not OK) and the role(s) they, and other people will play (victim, persecutor, rescuer). The script represents a childhood survival strategy. As adults, we are usually unaware of the script, yet many behaviours, feeling and thinking patterns frequently serve to live this unconscious script out to the final ending (Stewart and Joines 1987: 107).

The significance of scripts in terms of change is that when people are behaving in ways that on the surface appear self-defeating or painful (this may include addictive, unhealthy or negative behaviours), it may well be that they are acting out and reinforcing their script, rather than making adult choices. Two factors that Stewart and Joines (1987: 110) suggest may increase likelihood of a return to script behaviour are when:

1   The here-and-now situation is perceived as stressful by the person.

2   The here-and-now situation resembles a stressful situation from the person's childhood (referred to as a rubber-band situation or transference situation, where they unconsciously put the face of someone from their past onto someone else in the here and now, for example, the face of a parent onto a GP).

In stressful situations, the person has a choice to consciously respond as the adult they are and stay out of script (the power triangle, Figure 3.14), or unconsciously return to acting out a script decision (the drama triangle, Figure 3.13) they made when they were a vulnerable infant.

For example, upon being diagnosed with an illness, an individual may respond by accepting the diagnosis and then gathering information about the condition. They do this with the intention of doing something to help themselves manage the condition or recover (an adult position, regaining personal power). Alternatively, they may feel helpless and become depressed and remain stuck in this position (a child position), or they may blame others or external factors for their condition (a parent position).

In TA counselling and therapy, the life script would be explored so that the individual could develop a conscious awareness of their planned story and how they may unconsciously be setting up problem situations (playing games, etc.) and how these can be managed (to regain personal power). From this, the individual may learn how to manage, problem-solve and make choices as an adult, rather than reverting to any script behaviour (Stewart and Joines 1987: 111).

## Life positions

Every life script (including the games played) is based on one of four life positions (Berne, in Stewart and Joines. 1987: 117) and each time an individual responds from this position, they reinforce both the adopted life position and their script.

The four positions are:

1  I'm OK, you're OK (healthy, assertive and respectful)
2  I'm OK, you're not OK (Persecutor role, aggressive and blaming)
3  I'm not OK, you're OK (Victim role, passive, overly compassionate)
4  I'm not OK, you're not OK (futile role, manipulative or passive-aggressive)

NB: Characteristics of different life positions and the impact on communication are explored in the chapter on communication.

## Games and rackets

Games and rackets are unauthentic ways of communicating based on scripts and life positions. Steiner (1997) suggests that if you watch people and listen to the conversations they have, you will often notice a 'theme'. Communication that leaves people feeling good is usually game-free. Alternatively, communication that leaves people feeling depressed, sad, angry or scared usually indicates that a game has been played (Steiner 1997: 121).

Most people have a specific communication style and these patterns of communication link specifically to the life position they adopt (I'm OK, you're OK, etc.). In his book, *Games People Play*, Eric Berne explains a range of games and their impact on the players. When games are played people play the role of Victim (I'm not OK, you're OK), Rescuer (I'm OK, you're not OK and I'll make you OK) or Persecutor (I'm OK, you're not OK).

When people communicate un-authentically, hide their true feelings and do not take responsibility for their communication, it is suggested that they are playing a game. This is most often an unconscious process; people play games without realising they are playing them.

One obvious game that may occur in a helping relationship is the 'Why don't you – yes but' game:

Person: I need to …
Helper: Why don't you …
Person: Yes but …
Helper: Why don't you …
Person: Yes but …
Helper: Why don't you …
Person: Yes but … etc.

Reinforcement of script is the aim of the game. The outcome of the 'yes but' game is that after many 'yes but' responses, the helper, who is playing the role of rescuer, runs out of options and there is a period of silence. The helper (Rescuer) may then feel at a loss (Victim) and may move to feeling frustrated and blaming or berating the person (Persecutor role). Similarly, the person being helped may decide they could not rely on this person for help (and thus become the Persecutor). The role-switching indicates the commencement of the drama triangle, which serves only to reinforce the life position (OK, not OK).

### Drama triangle

The drama triangle is based on the three roles people can play when they are in game or script mode – the Victim, Rescuer or Persecutor roles. (NB: the use of capital letters is to denote a role, rather than a real situation where the person may actually be a victim, persecutor or rescuer.)

When people play games, they are usually acting out a role depicted by the life script they adopt with the aim being to reinforce the script and life position; they are not responding in ways that will help them to make changes; they are reacting in ways that help to keep them stuck. In the drama triangle, there is a shift between roles, the 'players' may begin the drama from one role and position and end in another position (James and Jongeward 1996: 87). People will move between roles when they act out the drama triangle (it is an unconscious process). They may start by playing a Rescuer and then become a Persecutor (if the person does not do what they want) and they may also end up in a Victim role, when the person they are helping rejects their rescuing.

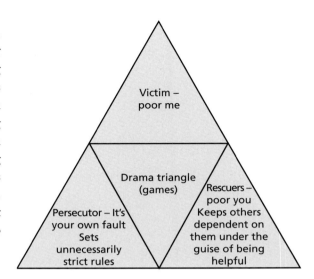

**Figure 3.13** The drama triangle

### Autonomy and power triangle

The goal of TA therapy is to build an individual's autonomy and personal power. That is, moving them out of any script behaviour and instead helping them to learn how to respond with 'awareness, spontaneity and the capacity for intimacy' (Stewart and Joines 1987: 6).

The power triangle is an alternative to the drama triangle. A person has personal power when 'they can bring about what they seek and prevent what they don't want' (Steiner 1997: 194). They 'are powerless when [they] cannot control what [they] eat, drink or put into [their] bodies, cannot sleep or stay awake or cannot think clearly or control their emotions or can't curb other people's controlling or oppressive behaviour' (Steiner 1997: 194).

Learning how to communicate assertively (discussed in Chapter 6) is a way forward for building personal power and response-ability.

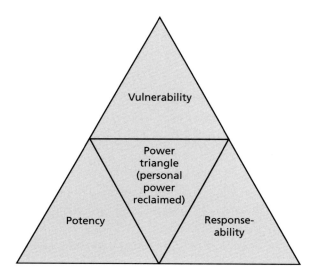

**Figure 3.14** The power triangle

Powerlessness is learned. External mistreatment (prejudice and 'ism's) can be introjected (projected inwards) so that the person ends up mistreating himself or herself. Self-determination comes from the use of 'personal non-abuse power' – or charisma (Steiner 1997: 196). This includes, being willing to own (response-ability) and express authentic feelings (vulnerability), for example, 'I feel hurt/sad/angry', etc., and communicate these assertively to bring about the changes one desires (potency).

In TA, the process of personal growth and change requires movement towards the 'I'm OK, you're OK' position where the person can respond authentically.

# MOTIVATIONAL INTERVIEWING

Motivational interviewing is defined as a 'client centred, directive method for enhancing intrinsic motivation to change by exploring and resolving ambivalence' (Miller and Rollnick 2002: 25). It was developed in the 1980s as a brief intervention targeting people with alcohol problems. Subsequent to this, it has been developed and used with clients for behaviour change in a variety of health areas. Motivational interviewing seeks to support the client to explore their behaviour, identify motivation for change, resolve ambivalence and decide a course of action. For the coach it involves listening deeply and attentively, letting the client speak and hear their own voice (thoughts, feelings) and guiding the person to explore themselves and their values and beliefs (out loud) with the aim of empowering the client. As Rollnick et al (2008: 10) suggest: 'A patient who is active in consultation, thinking aloud about the why and how of change, is more likely to do something about it afterwards.'

At its core, motivational interviewing has four processes:

1 Engaging – building rapport, listening and gaining a clear understanding of the issues and the clients perspective.
2 Focusing – narrowing the issues towards a specific goal.
3 Evoking – developing commitment to change, increasing commitment and confidence.
4 Planning – determining action to be taken.

In approaching motivational interviewing, the coach uses a range of communication skills including open questioning, reflective or active listening, affirming (making positive statements) and summarising (see Section 2). The coach may also provide information to inform the client but this is done sensitively in a non-judgemental manner, with permission from the patient, to support understanding and choice (see Section 1).

The skilled motivational interviewer will seek to identify, evoke and reinforce 'change talk' and sensitively steer the client away from the use of sustain talk (talk that reinforces staying with the current behaviour). 'Change talk' describes where a client expresses some form of intention to change; examples are seen in the table below.

The first four examples in Table 3.7 describe when people are considering change whereas the last two often are discussed as commitment increases and client start to make changes.

Sustain talk also revolves round the change, however, it differs from change talk in that it focuses on why the client 'cannot' change. It is important for the practitioner to recognise each type, as focusing on sustain talk can reinforce the current behaviour and move the client away from change. For example:

Client: I want to start exercising to help reduce my weight (change talk) but I just love my evenings in front of the telly (sustain talk).

Practitioner response 1: Tell me what you like about watching television? (Focusing on the sustain talk, likely to reinforce the fun of being a couch potato.)

Practitioner response 2: So you want to lose weight, tell me about your reasons for doing that. (Focusing on the change talk and helping the client focus on the benefits of losing weight.)

| Table 3.7 | Anticipating and managing lapses |
|---|---|
| **Theme** | **Example** |
| Desire – indicates a client's wish to make a change | I want to be thin; I wish I took more exercise; I like the idea of getting fit. I hope to cycle more to work; I will try to be more active. |
| Ability – indicates a client's perception of their ability | I could walk to the bus stop; I think I can fit in a gym session this week; I might be able to join a gym. |
| Reasons – indicates a client's reason for change | I would probably feel better if I was more active; I want to be independent in my old age. |
| Need – indicates a client's need or the necessity for change | I must get fitter; I have got to lose weight; I really should walk the kids to school each day. |
| Commitment – indicates a client's level of commitment to change | I will lose weight; I promise to run four times a week. Lower levels of commitment may include: I will take the dog for a walk in the mornings. |
| Actions/steps taken | I have bought a pair of trainers; I looked into a gym membership; I have been out for a walk this week. |

Adapted from Rollnick et al (2008: 37)

The role of the motivational interviewer is to help the client recognise change talk and build on it to strengthen commitment. Then, when the client is ready, the interviewer can guide the client towards determining an action plan and elicit commitment.

## SUMMARISING

A key communication skill from motivational interviewing is summarising, which is used once the coach has collected information from the client. A skilful summariser is able to draw together the main themes from the conversation and pull them together in such a way that highlights an understanding of the key issues and also shines a light on any change talk or positive moves towards change. Summarising enables the coach to show they have been listening, check if anything has been missed and emphasise positive aspects of what has been said.

## ADVICE-GIVING

As mentioned in the introduction to this section, the coach may choose to give information and advice to the client, but it has to be done in a client-centred manner. Rollnick et al (1999) recommend using the following approach:

• Determine what the client already knows and what they want or need to know.
• Make the distinction between factual information and personal interpretation of this information – the client should add meaning to the facts.
• Present information in a neutral manner.
• Use the elicit – provide – elicit process. This means asking the client if they would like the information; provide information neutrally, avoiding the term 'you', in language that the

person will understand, and ensuing comprehension moving from general to specific; elicit the patient's interpretation of the information.

Summarising and advice giving are discussed further in Section 3.

# SOLUTION-FOCUSED BRIEF THERAPY

Solution-focused brief therapy was developed in the 1980s by Steve de Shazer and Kim Berg, who were social workers working with families. 'It is, at its simplest, a conversation between therapist and client which in itself may help to provide a different experience of a problem and therefore uncover possible solutions that were not, and possibly could not, be considered previously' (Duncan et al 2007: 12). The central principles of solution-focused therapy are that the client chooses the goals for the session, and the client has the resources to make changes. Solution-focused therapy differs from many other therapies in that no detailed history is taken as the focus of the sessions is on solutions and starting something new, rather than focusing on problems and something that has already happened (MacDonald 2011: 8). It seeks to focus on the person rather than the problem, explore people's resources, their preferred future and ways to achieve it. As in motivational interviewing, the principle of the client as the expert with the ability to resolve their own problems is key.

The therapy uses similar techniques to motivational interviewing and NLP in terms of building rapport and questioning, but varies in the level of discussion of the problem, while goal-setting may be less specific. Solution-focused therapy uses a more structured approach as described below.

### First session
- Introductions.
- Problem-free talk – focusing on something the client enjoys or skill they possess.
- Determining the client's best hopes for the session.
- Discussing preferred future and what it will look like when the problem has been resolved.
- Scaling – where are they currently in relation to their goal and/or use of the 'miracle question'.

- Feedback – positive compliments, picking out skills, abilities and examples where they have been successful.
- Asking them to notice any changes.
- Ask if they want another session.

### Subsequent sessions
- Elicit – Assessing any changes (what is better) since last time.
- Amplify – more details of what is better and what exceptions there have been.
- Reinforce – compliments and encouragement.
- Start again – repeat the above until no more improvements are needed.
- Scaling – where are they now and what will they do next (adapted from MacDonald 2011).

## OVERVIEW OF CHANGE INTERVENTIONS

| Intervention | Key factors | Useful for | Implications for practice |
| --- | --- | --- | --- |
| CBT | Irrational beliefs ABC model Negative automatic thoughts (NATs) Schemas | Reviewing the influence of thinking patterns on behaviour Helps to reframe responses to relapse and setbacks | Need to be qualified as CBT counsellor Many self-help approaches (books, tools) are based on components from CBT |
| NLP | Matching and mirroring Questioning Language Goal-setting and visualising positive outcomes | Rapport-building Challenging language and thinking Visualising change | There are a large range of techniques used in NLP that support behaviour change. Further study through reading or attending courses is recommended |

| Intervention | Key factors | Useful for | Implications for practice |
|---|---|---|---|
| Transactional analysis | Parent, adult, child (PAC model) Drama triangle Power triangle OK philosophy | Identifying the impact of communication (with self and others) on behaviour Recognising ways in which the individual gives away personal power to make changes | Need to be qualified as TA counsellor |
| Motivational interviewing | Engaging Focusing Evoking Planning Reflective listening Change talk/sustain talk Summarising | Allowing the client to think out loud Exploring change and sustain talk Helping the client move towards what they want | Effective motivational interviewing demands great skill and professional training and ongoing development will be needed to practise effectively |
| Solution-focused | Best hopes Preferred futures Possible solutions Resources Miracle questions Scales (1–10) | Encouraging clients to develop their own solutions and action plans/next steps | Needs skill to ensure appropriate questions are used to get the client to recognise their skills and abilities and focus on solutions |

# MANAGING LAPSES

As a practitioner, it is important to anticipate the possibility of lapses and plan coping strategies to help minimise their occurrence or effect.

## LAPSE, RELAPSE OR COLLAPSE

Relapse and returning to old behaviours is always a risk for anyone making efforts to change. A useful strategy is, in the early stages of change, to identify the situations where the person will be most at risk of relapsing. Once the high-risk situation has been identified, strategies can be put in place to either prevent (proactive) or manage (reactive) the situation. Relapse can destroy the will of those who start with the highest aspirations and best of intentions. It can trigger feelings of failure and push the person to return to their old behaviour, and can leave them feeling incompetent (a failure).

Strategies for promoting adherence and preventing relapse may include:

- Using appropriate goals and targets that are personal and relevant to the individual.
- Planning for high-risk situations (see Table 3.8).

- Making small changes gradually to minimise lapses.
- Reinforcing the positive benefits from change.
- Rewarding success with appropriate 'treats'.
- Viewing lapses as normal and temporary.
- Seeking positive support from friends and family.

| Table 3.8 | Managing lapses | | |
|-----------|-----------------|---|---|
| Situation: Upcoming holiday, Christmas, birthday, wedding, etc., where it may be hard to stick to new habits and where I will probably overeat/not exercise/drink too much, etc. | | | |
| **State** | **What it is** | **Reaction** | **Strategies** |
| Lapse | A temporary deviation, or lapse, from the new lifestyle behaviour | Oh well, it was fun but now it's over so back on track. I'm not going to be able to go to the gym so I'll find someone to go walking with. I'll plan my return to normal in advance and enjoy the 'break'. | Those with a strong internal locus of control will see this as an allowable and temporary (enjoyable) lapse. Plan for it by cutting back or down before or after the event, finding alternative activity options, e.g. walking, pacing alcohol intake, etc. Return to the new behaviour immediately and avoid relapse |
| Relapse | A more permanent return to a previous stage of change or old behaviour | Ate too much at the event so have blown it for this week. It wasn't my fault, people kept offering me … Will start again on Monday/next month/soon. | Relapse and collapse are often the result of a weak internal locus of control and highlight the need to plan before a high-risk event. Developing a stronger internal locus of control will help to develop a coping strategy to manage high-risk situations. |
| Collapse | A fall back to pre-contemplation or to an exacerbated form of the old behaviour with a few new bad habits as well | I was determined to stick to salad and mineral water but ended up eating and/or drinking too much at the event so I am a complete failure and I knew it would happen as I'm always a failure. Ends up back in the old lifestyle patterns but worse, eating more, drinking more, not exercising and regaining all and more of the weight lost. Regress to pre-contemplation with a sense of 'I knew it wouldn't work, no point in trying again, it's my genes …' | Take control and consider how to plan for and enjoy the lapse without affecting the overall lifestyle changes. Instead of intending to deny any 'bad' or enjoyable behaviours, plan to indulge a little and to enjoy it. Take control of the situation and reinforce the internal locus of control – 'I can …', 'I will …'. For example, if usual activity is not possible go for a brisk walk each day, alternate alcohol with water or eat the food on offer – just leave a third of it on the plate. |

## ABSTINENCE VIOLATION EFFECT

Commonly used in the treatment of addiction but applicable to lifestyle, the abstinence violation effect (AVE) is about the reaction to the violation (lapse) of abstinence (giving up), in this case negative lifestyle behaviours, that influences the probability of returning to the new positive behaviour or relapsing to the previous negative patterns. It can be applied to any desired change.

An individual with high or stable self-efficacy will see any lapse as the result of an external cause – for example, a holiday or Christmas – and be able to accept the lapse, maintain control and keep working towards the new goals. However, if self-efficacy is low, they are likely to feel guilty and conflicted and experience a sense of it being their fault. This can lead to one or more of the following reactions:

- Overgeneralising:
  - 'I'm a complete failure.'
  - 'Nothing ever goes right for me.'
  - 'I'm never going to be able to do this.'
- Selective-abstraction:
  - Focusing on the one small slip and not on any successes, which solidifies the sense of being a failure, for example, 'I ruined a week's good eating with that one biscuit …', 'Nineteen people liked it but one person didn't – I knew it wasn't good enough …'
- Creating a self-fulfilling prophecy, for example, 'I always fail', 'I told you I couldn't do this'.
- Excessive responsibility:
  - 'It's all my fault.'
  - 'I'm useless.'
  - 'No one can help me.'
- Catastrophising:
  - Exaggerating the slip, for example, 'This is the worst possible thing that could ever happen', 'I can't imagine anything worse'.
  - Seeing no possibility of success in the future, ever, for example, 'I will never succeed so I may as well give up'.

A typical example is the 'Monday dieter' – the person who starts a new diet every Monday but manages to lapse with a biscuit at elevenses, prompting the response of 'Well, I've blown it now so I might as well forget about it until next Monday'. Sound familiar?

## SUMMARY

Lapses are an unavoidable factor in change and as such should be acknowledged, managed and used to predict future triggers or events that may crop up. Pretending they have not or will not occur is like ignoring the hole in the pavement – and falling in! Part of the role of any practitioner involved in change is helping clients to understand and accept this.

### KEY POINTS

- Models of change are many and varied.
- Similarly, theories come in many shapes and sizes, much like clients.
- No one model has the right fit for any one client.
- Models and theories are often spiral or cyclical rather than linear.
- There are a range of interventions that can be used with clients to support behaviour change.
- The client is the expert on themselves, however, they may need support in realising this.

# LEARNING THEORIES

## 4

A theory of how people learn is a crucial component of any approach intended to help people make changes. Once again, there are numerous theorists contributing ideas regarding how people learn (behaviourists, cognitivists, humanists, etc.). A basic introduction is provided here, while reference sources that provide further information are acknowledged throughout.

Most human behaviours and actions can be attributed to the process of learning. We learn:

- Helpful knowledge, attitudes and behaviours (how and why to cross the road safely).
- Skilful knowledge, attitudes and behaviours (how and why to drive a car and how to play a sport).
- Healthy and unhealthy knowledge, attitudes and behaviours (how and why to choose the food we eat and the habits we engage or do not engage with, including inactivity).

Learning has occurred when there is an almost permanent change of behaviour that affects and influences three main learning domains:

1   Skills: What a person does, their actions and behaviours (psychomotor).

2   Knowledge: How a person thinks, their beliefs and thinking (cognitive).
3   Attitude: How a person feels, their values (affective).

For example, if a primary value is being healthy (attitude) and a person knows what behaviours constitute being healthy (knowledge) and how to undertake these behaviours (skill), then they are more likely to actively engage with these behaviours. Alternatively, if a person lacks a certain skill or piece of knowledge or if their value base is different (e.g. if health is not a primary focus), then they are less likely to prioritise or engage with some behaviours.

## LEARNING STYLES

There are many theories that contribute to the study of how people learn, what they do and what they feel (knowledge, skills and attitude). VAK (visual, auditory, kinaesthetic) is one model that describes learning styles. The significance of this is then how the practitioner chooses to work with the person (see Table 4.1). Very basically, a person who has a visual learning preference will take in information that is visual – so any health messages and advice may need to be given in a way that they can see (leaflets, posters, etc.). An individual who has a stronger auditory preference, may need to listen to and discuss different health messages with someone (such as a GP). A kinaesthetic learner will prefer to learn by physically doing something. In reality, we all use a combination of senses to take in information, so from a learning perspective (and when helping people to make changes) it is useful to provide information through all of these channels.

The Chinese philosopher Confucius developed the proverb: 'I hear and I forget. I see and I remember. I do and I understand.' The proverb infers that learning does not come from listening alone or simply watching. It comes from engaging with something, experiencing it and integrating it. The 'doing' or kinaesthetic aspect can be a neglected area in some helping environments, which means a key way in which people learn is not being maximised. A simple way of engaging this style (and it may not work for all people) would be, during a consultation, asking them to record their own 'data' (for example, completing a questionnaire, letting someone take their own heart rate and/or even writing down and recording any data used for monitoring changes, such as their blood pressure reading, heart rate, etc.).

| Table 4.1 | Learning preferences | |
|---|---|---|
| **Sensory learning preference** | **Characteristics** | **Learn by** |
| Visual 'See' | Learn through visual awareness – observing and watching (this may include reading). | Watching others. Reading books and handouts. Seeing posters, advertisements and charts. Stimulated by pictures, colour, images and visual displays and resources. |
| Auditory/aural 'Hear' | Learn through auditory/aural awareness – speaking, listening and hearing. | Speaking and asking questions. Listening to others provide information. Listening to audio recordings. Discussion with others. Asking questions and listening to answers. Attending talks. |
| Kinaesthetic 'Do' | Learn through kinaesthetic awareness – doing something, moving, actively taking part and feeling the experience. | Doing something physically. Working with others. Trying something and experiencing it, finding out what it feels like. Taking part and practising. Making notes. |

## STAGES OF LEARNING AND DEVELOPMENT

There are three stages to learning (Fitts and Posner 1967, in Reece and Walker 2003 and Davis et al 2005). These stages are:

1  The cognitive phase
2  The fixative or associative phase
3  The autonomous phase

The process of learning is the same for healthy and unhealthy behaviours. In order to learn something or change or correct learned behaviour (relearn), an individual has to go back to an earlier stage of the learning process and bring the learning process (thinking, doing, feeling) back into their conscious awareness once again.

## SUMMARY

In order to change, an individual would need to have *learned* something. There is arguably no change without some form of learning taking place. The texts referenced throughout this chapter provide a valuable resource for further exploration of the many theories and models applied to human learning, motivation and attitude and behaviour change.

| Table 4.2 | Stages of learning | |
|-----------|--------------------|---|
| **Phase** | **Level of awareness/ability** | **Learned by** |
| Cognitive | Knowing how to do something – watching, listening and thinking about how something is done (a conscious process). Short-term learning. | Observation. Watching others. Listening to others. Role-modelling. Reading instructions. |
| Fixative/ associative | Acquiring the behaviour patterns – engaging with, and practising the action or behaviour (a conscious process). Learning achieved over a longer period of time. | Doing something. Practice. Repetition. Experience. Feedback from others that reinforces the behaviour. |
| Autonomous | Behaviour becomes automatic and organised – there is less cognitive control (e.g. an unconscious process, not thinking about what doing). Learning is ingrained/automatic. | Habitual patterns. Feedback or stimuli that help to trigger, reinforce and refine the behaviour. |

## KEY POINTS

- There are many theories of learning and, again, no one theory provides a 'best fit'.
- Much of our behaviour is learned from others or unconsciously, and whether positive or negative, healthy or unhealthy, these behaviours can be hard to break.
- Learning styles can affect absorption of knowledge and behaviour patterns.
- Stages of learning are threefold: consciously learning; consciously practising; unconsciously doing.
- Good and bad behaviours can be changed.

# SECTION TWO

## THE SKILLS

### INTRODUCTION

In Section 1, we considered the background and underpinning knowledge of behaviour change. Section 2 looks at the process of change, the role of communication in helping facilitate change and identifies key tools and strategies that the practitioner can use.

Knowing and understanding the theories and models that are used to predict or explain behaviour or the process of change is good, understanding the different interventions is helpful, but being able to put it into practice is the most important factor in assisting change. As previously discussed, people are not (theoretical) model-shaped and theories don't always fit, so the 'what' is less relevant to the practitioner than the 'how to' of change. The way we ask a question or the way we listen to the answer are important here; get it wrong and it can lead to resistance, get it right and it opens the door to change and success.

The focus here is on the skills that are useful when assisting individuals in lifestyle behaviour change. The aim of this section is to:

- Discuss the needs of the client and the psychology of change.
- Outline the client-centred approach/person-centred working.
- Identify barriers to making changes for the individual.
- Identify barriers to helping that the helper/practitioner may encounter.
- Review professional boundaries and limits.
- Review goal-setting, including process and outcome goals, such as SMART, $P^4$.

### LEARNED HEALTH BEHAVIOUR

Before we start, take time to consider your own health behaviours, are they positive or negative or a mix of both; what or who has helped shape them? How did you learn these behaviours?

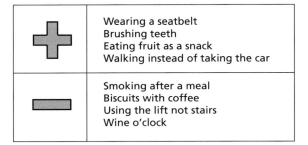

| | |
|---|---|
| **+** | Wearing a seatbelt<br>Brushing teeth<br>Eating fruit as a snack<br>Walking instead of taking the car |
| **—** | Smoking after a meal<br>Biscuits with coffee<br>Using the lift not stairs<br>Wine o'clock |

**Figure 5.1** Health behaviours

Just as our general behaviour develops over time and through various influencing factors, so our health behaviour is influenced by a variety of factors. For example, if we observe our parents smoking, we are more likely to smoke and if we are fed a healthy diet as children, we are more likely to be healthy eaters as adults.

Learned health behaviours are likely to be firmly established and often have their roots in childhood, whether the behaviours are positive or negative. For this reason, changing behaviours is not simply a question of deciding to change and doing it. Habits, whether good or bad, are hard to break.

| Table 5.1 | Health Habits task | |
|---|---|---|
| Task: Think about your 'health' habits. Using the table below, make a note of where/when/who shaped these or helped you learn these | | |
| **Habit** | **Positive or negative?** | **Influenced by?** |
| | | |
| | | |
| | | |
| | | |
| | | |
| | | |
| | | |
| | | |

THE SKILLS

# THE PSYCHOLOGY OF CHANGE

5

The practitioner, whether a fitness instructor, exercise referral specialist or sports coach, has a significant role in facilitating change. It is important to understand not only the elements of the role but also the professional and personal limits and boundaries that need to be in place.

## CLIENT/PERSON-CENTRED APPROACH TO WORKING

The person-centred or client-centred approach evolves from the work of Carl Rogers, who believed that people are capable of working out their own solutions to their problems in the right environment. In a helping relationship, the right environment is one where the core conditions (empathy, congruence and unconditional positive regard) are present (these core conditions are discussed later).

Rogers (1967: 90) asserted that the 'person is the best expert on themselves' and within themselves they have the resources they need to bring about personal change. In the presence of the core conditions, the person is able to access their resources (Feltham and Horton 2000: 348) and choose their own values and standards and achieve their potential.

The sole motivation in the person-centred approach is the movement towards this fulfilment of potential. Each person develops a self-concept (me, myself, I) that represents their values, goals, ideals, how they perceive themselves and how they perceive their world and environment (Feltham and Horton 2000: 348). Some people may develop a healthy and accurate self-concept; others, more often may develop a self-concept that does not represent their true potential, which impacts their self-esteem and self-confidence, consider, for example, the story of the ugly duckling.

Rogers believed that: 'Many adult adjustment problems are bound up by attempts to live by other people's standards rather than ones' own' (in Gross 1996: 764). People are born and begin life as *congruent* (true to themselves), but as they grow and experience rejection and/or disapproval (like the ugly duckling), they become *conditioned* by the negative experiences and these *'conditions of worth'* are internalised as part of their *self-concept* (e.g. I only have worth if I behave, think, feel in a certain way that meets the approval of those around me), they then lose sight of their potential. Rogers believed that motivation and behaviour were a response, by the individual, that related to their perception and interpretation of external stimuli from the environment. An individual may develop a self-concept that is incongruent and not connected to their true self and the incongruent self-concept becomes dependent on reinforcement from others to maintain self-esteem and self-worth. 'Anxiety, threat and confusion are created whenever incongruence is experienced between the self-concept, with its internalised conditions of worth, and actual experience' and the resulting behaviour may be 'destructive, disorganized and chaotic' (Feltham and Horton, 2000).

Examples of incongruence exist when a person longs to do something but feels it is not appropriate for them to do it, because of their conditioned beliefs. For example, if a girl is brought up to believe that football is a boys' game, and 'young ladies, do not play sports', then she may deny the part of herself that longs to play football. Or a boy who is conditioned to believe that dancing is for girls may deny the part of himself that longs to dance. Similarly, an individual who develops an addictive behaviour may have lost their sense of self-value and worth; their behaviour may be a way of coping in an environment that, deep down, they find harsh and unwelcoming.

The role of the helper is to create an environment where the client feels accepted and valued for who they are, and in which any fear of being judged or condemned is minimised. When the person experiences this environment (the core conditions), they feel safe to speak openly and honestly, with no need to deny, distort or withhold information about themselves. This enables them to explore themselves and their thoughts, and, from this, acceptance, change and growth can happen.

## THE CORE CONDITIONS

In the person-centred approach, the person is the centre of the process. The helper or practitioner builds a positive relationship with the person that maintains the presence of the three primary core conditions:

1 Unconditional positive regard.
2 Empathy.
3 Congruence.

The presence of these conditions will enable successful change. No other strategies or tools would be used by person-centred practitioners, unless these were requested by the person they are working with. The main focus is building the relationship and reflecting back to the person the feelings, experiences, bodily sensations and thoughts they share, so that a greater understanding of who they are can be developed.

### Unconditional positive regard

Unconditional positive regard is about acceptance and showing respect and warmth for the person. It is about prizing them as an individual in their own right, valuing the way they manage their struggles, appreciating their own unique way of being and valuing who they are without judgement or making decisions that they should be any other way.

It is fairly normal for human beings to dislike and judge certain human behaviours and to have prejudices. However, in order to demonstrate unconditional positive regard, one needs to be aware of these tendencies and take responsibility for processing these judgements as a growing aspect of self. These judgements should not be used to condemn or disempower another person.

Someone working as a counsellor would take these issues to their supervision, however, instructors and coaches may not have that form of line management.

## Empathy

Empathy is seeing things from the other person's perspective, putting yourself into their position and understanding their world as if it were your own, without losing the 'as if' quality (Rogers 1967: 93). To be empathic, the practitioner needs to put to one side any need to analyse and evaluate, as this serves only to see the person's world from their own perspective. Empathy is building an understanding of how the person sees their world – it is their map, it is not about agreeing or disagreeing (judging), it is developing an appreciation of how things are for them.

Sanders (1997: 66) suggests that to be empathic the practitioner needs to:

* Listen sensitively.
* Aim to make sense of what they hear.
* Understand the other person from their frame of reference.
* Check to see if they have understood correctly.

Active listening and other communication skills are of key importance for developing empathy. Giving the person space to tell their story and using reflective statements and paraphrasing will mirror empathy. These skills are explored further in Chapter 6.

Empathy is powerful, as Rogers (1967: 93) states: 'When someone understands how it feels and seems to be to me, without wanting to analyse me or judge me, then I can blossom and grow in that climate.'

## Congruence

Congruence is being honest, genuine and presenting the whole self, without putting on a front or a façade/mask. A practitioner who mirrors congruence will enable the client to do the same. When an individual is able to get in touch with their own authentic feelings and thoughts, rather than denying these aspects of self, and be accepted, they learn to value themselves 'warts and all'. Positive self-regard is no longer dependent on conditions of worth (Gross 1996: 764).

To be congruent, the practitioner needs to be aware of their own thoughts and feelings and manage these, without denying or discounting them. They may choose to communicate these thoughts or feelings, if appropriate. Most people are able to sense incongruence, when a person is putting on a front to perform a role. People can also recognise when a person is not communicating the things they think or feel and thus will often hold back from revealing themselves at any deeper level. Alternatively, with a person who is authentic, people are more likely to develop trust and be more of who they are as a consequence.

However, congruence should not be confused with the need to 'blurt out impulsively every feeling and accusation under the comfortable impression that one is being genuine' (Rogers 1967: 91) as this is not helpful! (See also assertive communication in Chapter 6.)

For example: a practitioner may work with a client who constantly lapses from their activity and healthy eating plan, which may lead to feelings of frustration and possibly annoyance on the part of the practitioner. In most instances, it would not be helpful for the exercise professional to tell the client how frustrated they feel, as the client may feel scolded and become disheartened. A more helpful strategy may be to demonstrate active listening and ask the client how they feel about the lapse and what this means for or to them.

An essential aspect of congruence is learning to communicate effectively. We communicate emotions and attitudes to others not only with the words (7 per cent) we use, but also through our intonation (38 per cent) and body language (55 per cent) (Petty 2004). Clearly, any discrepancy between what we say and how we feel will be communicated at some level. The response we get from our communication may actually tell us more about what we are communicating than what we say, or how we say it. Communication skills are explored further in Chapter 6.

## SUMMARY

The person-centred approach is about building a relationship and developing an open channel for communication. It is about facilitating an environment where the person can explore what works for them and what fits with who they are and their lifestyle.

It is not about telling someone what to do, making judgements about them or dictating what is right for them (even if the advice is sound). Person-centred working is putting the person at the centre of the process and letting them find their own way in their own time. It is not a quick fix approach to working and often requires longer-term contact with the client. Many other helping approaches embrace the core conditions as the foundation for their work, the difference being that other approaches include the use of other tools and strategies within their work (such as CBT).

| Table 5.2 | Person-centred vs. non-person-centred approaches |
| --- | --- |
| **Person-centred approach** | **Non-person-centred approach** |
| Being empathic | Being unconcerned about their struggles |
| Being unbiased | Being judgemental, which includes making judgements, blaming or giving self-righteous opinions in relation to their choices (including lifestyle behaviours, use of alcohol, smoking, eating, inactivity, etc.) |
| Being supportive | Being dismissive |
| Being accepting | Finding fault and blaming |
| Being optimistic | Being sceptical |
| Letting the person lead the process and make decisions | Directing and dictating the process |

Adapted from Waine (2002)

## KEY POINTS

- Assisting change needs a person- or client-centred approach.
- Communication and rapport-building are key in this approach.
- The core conditions of unconditional positive regard, empathy and congruence are the key factors in positive and successful relationships with clients.
- Unconditional positive regard is showing acceptance and respect for the client without judging them or trying to change who they are.
- Empathy is seeing things from the client's perspective.
- Congruence is simply showing understanding to the client.
- Demonstrating core conditions when communicating may require the practitioner to examine and put aside their own feelings so they can work in a client-centred way.
- At the core, the practitioner is not trying to change the client, merely help them with changing behaviours.

# COMMUNICATION SKILLS

**6**

Good communication is a vital skill when working with clients in all areas of fitness, activity and sport. It is also a valuable skill in everyday life, as it can help with personal as well as professional relationships. Communication skills are often taken for granted, yet poor communication can be at the root of many misunderstandings and issues, while good communication can avoid or minimise problems and boost relationships, professional and personal.

The aims of this chapter are:

- To provide an overview of a range of communication skills including:
  - Listening
  - Questioning
  - Observation
  - Reflecting
  - Summarising
  - Verbal and non-verbal communication routes.
- To discuss the use of communication skills in building rapport and identifying a client's true motivation and beliefs.

## BUILDING RAPPORT

For a professional to be successful in supporting behaviour change it is first vital that they build a rapport with the client. There a variety of ways of building rapport but neurolinguistic programming (NLP) uses a number of techniques that can assist this process.

One such technique is 'matching and mirroring' – in effect, copying the person. Matching is copying on the same side and mirroring is copying the opposite side. But matching does not have to be confined to copying movements – there are other elements that can be copied as follows:

1. Physiology – posture, facial expressions, breathing.
2. Voice – tone, speed, volume, pitch and rhythm.
3. Language – key words or representational systems. People tend to favour using expressions that are either visually, auditory or kinaesthetically focused.

For example, a person who favours visual language will use terms such as 'it appears to me', 'the future looks bright', or 'I see what you mean', while people who favour auditory language will use expressions such as 'I hear that', 'that sounds good to me', or 'that is music to my ears' and kinaesthetic people will use expressions that involve movement or feelings, such as 'I feel that', 'get to grips with' or 'the overall feeling is ...'.

The following exercise is from *Whispering in the Wind* by Richard Grinder and Carmen Bostic St Clair (2001):

1   For 30 seconds, slowly move the bottom half of your body to the same position as your client, adjusting your position to match any movements.
2   For the next 30 seconds, subtly move the upper part of your body to the same position as your client.
3   In the third 30 seconds, position your head with the same tilt both side to side and front to back, and imitate certain facial expressions.
4   In the next 30 seconds, match the frequency, depth and timing of your clients breathing.
5   Test that you have achieved rapport by slowly moving a portion of your body to a new position and see if the client shifts to that position without conscious awareness. If not, return to step 1.

## EFFECTIVE LISTENING

Listening is a skill that requires practice. Listening with the intention to hear the person fully demands not only using the ears but also watching (observing body language) and using intuition to hear the real meaning of and fully understand what the person is saying (reading between the lines). 'Listening in the counselling sense is done with the head, heart and gut' as well as the eyes and ears (Ellin 1994: 41), and should happen in the presence of the core conditions

– unconditional positive regard, empathy and congruence (see the discussion of the person-centred approach in Chapter 5).

Learning to listen helpfully requires the development of an awareness to pick up on everything that is happening. It requires attention be paid to the many areas that provide information, which include, as Ellin (1994: 44) suggests:

• What is being said.
• The facts.
• Words used.
• Body language.
• Voice intonation, volume and rhythm.
• Feelings spoken and unspoken.
• The environment.
• How relaxed or tense the person is.
• Own feelings and thoughts.
• Any personal distress activated through listening.

Another important aspect of listening is giving respect to any silences. Although silence can sometimes feel uncomfortable, it may indicate that the person is processing information, such as 'thinking deeply, experiencing an old feeling or even pondering an insight that may not be ready to share' (Ellin 1994: 43). At these times, it is useful if the helper is able to hold the silence and at the same time hold the thoughts, feelings and insights that may be being experienced, rather than cutting in and blocking the experience.

Listening will also enable you to gain clues about the learning style of the client. People often use words that link to their preferred style, as outlined above, and if you can identify these it can make the way you communicate more effective. Typical words and phrases used by different styles are illustrated in Table 6.1.

| Table 6.1 | Learning styles and listening | | |
|---|---|---|---|
| **Situation** | **Visual** | **Auditory** | **Kinaesthetic** |
| Listening to a client | I see what you mean | I hear what you are saying | I know how you feel |
| Planning a programme | Write a programme card | Ask for verbal instructions, use an mp3 player | Complete the programme according to what feels good |
| Checking understanding | Do you see what I mean? | Do you hear what I mean? | Do you get what I mean? |
| Clarifying instructions | Can I see that again? Show me how to … | Can you say that again? Tell me how to … | Can I have a go? Let me try … |
| Demonstrating or teaching | Say 'watch me do it' Give written instructions | Say 'listen to the instructions' Give a verbal explanation | Say 'you have a go' Give a demonstration |
| Setting up new equipment | Read the instructions | Get someone to read the instructions out | Give it a go |
| Buy or try a new product | Read reviews | Discuss with others | Go and try it out |
| Would prefer | Books | Music | Gadgets |

Active and effective listening can be demonstrated in the following ways:

- Acknowledgement: Making some acknowledgement as the person speaks, such as nodding the head, maintaining eye contact, saying 'yes' or making another sound of acknowledgement ('ummm', 'uh huh', etc.).
- Reflecting back what the person says – for example, Client: 'I feel depressed.' Practitioner: 'You feel depressed.' – or reading between the lines and making a guess at what they are communicating with the aim of keeping them moving by using reflective statements – for example, Client: 'I am worried about my drinking.' Practitioner: 'You are drinking more and this worries you.' NB: be careful of the tone of your voice, as an inclination in the voice at the end of a statement can turn it into a question and may have a different effect. This can be a problem if your native language or dialect has a natural rise or fall at the end of sentences so it may be helpful to record a session and listen to how your tone may be interpreted. Be careful to use the client's words, not complex or confrontational ones.
- Asking questions to clarify what the client is saying, for example, 'Tell me more about feeling depressed.'

## BARRIERS TO LISTENING

Even when we think we listen attentively, we need to be aware of other blocks to listening. These include:

- Relating everything to yourself and your own experience. This takes the focus off the person and back to you.
- Thinking about the next question you want to ask your client. If you are spending time thinking about your next question, you are not listening to what they are saying in the here and now! You may also be switching off to some vital information they are giving you.
- Switching off and letting your mind daydream as the person speaks. If this happens, it is far more respectful to apologise, acknowledge what has happened and ask the client to repeat what they were saying.
- Making internal judgements on what the client has said. Judging them as unmotivated, lazy, a complainer, a nuisance or any other judgement will block listening.
- Interrupting and giving advice. For example, if the client says they struggle to find time to exercise, telling them what they should do to make time is not hearing the struggle they present. It is more helpful to acknowledge the struggle they present and then ask if they would like to explore different ways to overcome their struggle. It may be that they do not want to, or are not ready to change.
- Ignoring any expression of emotion and responding with shallow, unempathic comments, such as 'well, we all find that difficult' or 'it could be worse'. These comments draw attention away from what the person is experiencing and are quite dismissive.

Exploration of these emotions may be crucial for identifying ways for them to move forward and resolve the issues presented for positive change.

Further blocks to listening may include personal factors such as:

- Tiredness and personal stress.
- Individual differences (culture, gender, age, etc.).
- Having experiences too similar to those the person is presenting and thus relating everything back to yourself.
- Being unable to relate to their experience. For example, if you do not have children, it may be more difficult to understand the time issues of a person who complains about not having time to exercise because they have children.

Twelve responses that are also potential roadblocks and evidence of not listening reflectively (Gordon 1970, in Rollnick and Miller 1991: 73) include:

1 Ordering, directing, or commanding (e.g. 'You must do this to improve your health').
2 Warning or threatening (e.g. 'You could die early if you don't do this').
3 Giving advice, making suggestions or providing solutions (e.g. 'If I were you, I would do it this way, it always works for me').
4 Persuading with logic, arguing, or lecturing (e.g. 'You know this makes sense, I don't see why you won't do it').
5 Moralising, preaching, or telling clients what they 'should' do (e.g. 'You really should do this, it's important for your family and they will thank you').

6 Disagreeing, judging, criticising, or blaming (e.g. 'It is your fault you are in this position, no one forced you to be lazy').

7 Agreeing, approving, or praising (e.g. 'It is hard, so if you don't succeed, it doesn't matter', 'I know exactly what you mean').

8 Shaming, ridiculing, or labelling (e.g. 'Do you really want to be the only fat person in your family?').

9 Interpreting or analysing (e.g. 'I think you really mean that you can't be bothered').

10 Reassuring, sympathising or consoling (e.g. 'It must have been awful for you, no wonder you felt like eating all those biscuits, never mind it doesn't really matter').

11 Questioning or probing (e.g. 'Hang on, why did you say that? It doesn't make sense to me so can you explain it?').

12 Withdrawing, distracting, humouring, or changing the subject (e.g. 'Yes, well, anyway, I think we have talked enough about that so tell me about your weekend, what did you do?').

There may be a time and place for each of these responses. The key is to recognise that they are not reflective listening and may block the direction the client's communication was moving in and may take them in another direction, or sometimes block the conversation altogether (Rollnick and Miller 1991: 74).

# QUESTIONING

'The way a question is framed of phrased has a specific power and result' (Duncan et al 2007: 11). There are different types of questions that can be used to gather information. Questions should always be used sparingly and with the aim of opening up the conversation. Questions should always be followed by reflective listening rather than more questions as too many questions may create resistance and stop some people from speaking. Additionally, clients sometimes need time to think about an answer before putting it into words and a skilled communicator will allow for this.

| Table 6.2 | Types of questions | |
|---|---|---|
| **Type of question** | **Description and purpose** | **Example** |
| Open | Effective for opening a conversation and gathering information. Begin with the words: *What? Who? Where? Why? When? How?* | How are you feeling? What activities did you enjoy when you were younger? |
| Probing | To encourage the client to expand on an initial response | Tell me more about that? |
| Focusing | To inquire more closely about a specific response | Why does that happen? What is it that creates that feeling? |
| Closed | Usually encourage just a 'yes' or 'no' response. Less useful for gathering information. | Did that hurt? |

# CHANNELS OF COMMUNICATION

Communication is the process by which we both send and receive information and by which we can influence or be influenced by another person. For communication to be successful, it needs to be a two-way process, with both parties engaged and actively taking part in the process.

Petty (2004) suggests that the chain of communication involves the four stages shown in Figure 6.1. Any break or block within the communication chain may have significant effects on the message that is interpreted. The message sent and the message received may be affected by both conscious processes (those we are aware of) and unconscious processes (those that are out of our current awareness).

Any discrepancy between what we say and how we feel will usually be communicated one way or another. The response we get from our communication may actually tell us more about what we are communicating than what we say, or how we choose to express it, at a conscious level! The more conscious we can be of all our communication processes (including the body language we use) and the responses we receive from the recipient(s) of our communication, the more potential we have to develop our communication skills.

Mehabrian (in Boyes 2005: 16) suggested that around 93 per cent of our communication of emotions comes from non-verbal channels, which means we need to pay more attention to the *how* of what is being said than the *what*.

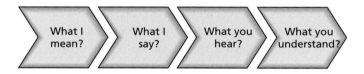

**Figure 6.1** Chain of communication

| Table 6.3 | Channels of communication (emotions/attitudes) | | |
|---|---|---|---|
| Channel of communication | Verbal – 7 per cent | Para-verbal – 38 per cent | Non-verbal – 55 per cent |
| Examples | What we say: Language we use; Words we speak or write; Jargon; Terminology; Learning style. | How we say things: Voice tone; Accent; Voice volume. | Body language: Posture and gestures; Eye contact and movements; Facial expressions; Proximity/closeness. |

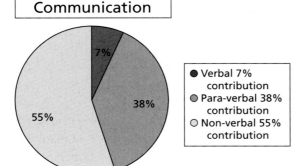

**Figure 6.2** Contribution of different channels to overall communication of emotions

## VERBAL COMMUNICATION
### Language

To promote effective communication we need to use vocabulary that is appropriate to the person with whom we are communicating. The language people are comfortable using may be related to their educational background, their social class, country of origin and the region they live in.

Simple, non-technical language is usually more accessible to everyone and is therefore most effective at communicating the message we want heard. The use of excessive terminology or intellectualising can be both confusing, intimidating, disorientating and alienating to some listeners, creating an instant block to the communication process. Colloquial or slang language should be avoided as it can be variously interpreted and may cause offence.

### Jargon

All professions have aspects of jargon. In the exercise and fitness environment, technical muscle names are used (e.g. pectorals instead of chest), muscle names are shortened (e.g. pecs or lats) and choreography may be given specific names. If a person is unfamiliar with the jargon, the intended message will not be communicated, which can be both frustrating and disheartening. The use of simple and accessible language and/or explaining jargon and any acronyms will assist communication.

### The written word

When we communicate verbally, the words we use, while important, are aided and amplified by the para-verbal and non-verbal elements of communication. When using words in their written form, these elements are missing so it can be easy to misinterpret communication. For example, the use of uppercase letters on a text or email can imply anger while exclamation marks are often used to minimise any negative impact of a message. Consider how you use the written word when communicating with clients as it is important to keep any message friendly and supportive and avoid upsetting someone with an inappropriate style of writing. If in doubt, wait and then reread before sending a written message or get someone else to read it first.

## PARA-VERBAL COMMUNICATION

An often overlooked aspect of communication is the element of para-verbal communication. This is related to how we say things, including tone of voice, volume and pitch, the emphasis we place on word.

### Voice volume and tone

Voice volume and intonation can reflect our interest/emotion. Voice volume will need to be adapted to suit specific environments so that what we say can be heard. A further consideration is that within different cultures/countries, volume and intonation can have a different meaning and effect. In the UK, shouting or speaking loudly can often be perceived as a sign of aggression and this can be distressing for some people. In some countries, for example India, quieter speech is accepted as a sign of politeness, while in others, such as some states of the USA, louder speech can be a more natural practice. Awareness of body language and facial expressions used with specific intonations will also impact on how communication is received.

## Emphasis

The emphasis we place on particular words or phrases in a sentence can alter the perceived meaning. Say the following examples aloud, placing emphasis on the word in italics and see if (and how) the meaning differs:

- *I* thought you would say that.
- I *thought* you would say that.
- I thought *you* would say that.
- I thought you *would* say that.
- I thought you would *say* that.
- I thought you would say *that*.

This is important, as often a person will place emphasis on the word or phrase that has most importance for them, even if it appears that something else is the 'official' reason for making changes. This means listening carefully to the way people say something is as important is listening to the words they are saying.

Consider the following, paying attention to the italicised phrases:

Practitioner: Tell me a little about why you want to make these changes

Client: Well, I really should do something to improve my health, I'm worried about my weight and getting diabetes, my mum has that and it's not good. I also should do something for my bones or so my doctor tells me. I ought to start taking more care of myself as I'm not getting any younger. *My school reunion is in six months and I'd really like to look good when I walk in.* I find stairs a bit harder so I tend to take the lift most of the time but that is not so good, is it? We are also going on holiday and I want to have enough energy to enjoy that *and look OK in a swimsuit.*

This client may know about the health benefits and risks, but from this conversation, her clear motivation is looking good for her school reunion and for the holiday. A good thing about physical activity is that the motivation for becoming more active is irrelevant to the outcome; it doesn't matter whether a client wants to exercise to reduce disease risk or to look good, the health benefits will occur regardless. However, the motivation to be active may be significantly improved if the end goal meets their inner desire, which for this client is looking good.

## Accent

In most countries and cultures, there are many and diverse regional accents. Words spoken can be shortened or pronounced differently with the emphasis on different letters or syllables, and there may even be different meanings of words. The main consideration for a person with a strong regional accent or who knowingly shortens words would be to consciously choose to speak slightly slower and attend to pronunciation to assist communication.

## BODY LANGUAGE – THE NON-VERBAL CHANNEL

Most of our body language is spontaneous and outside of our conscious awareness. It often transmits the 'truth' (congruency) in relation to what we are feeling or thinking on the inside. Boyes (2005: 9) suggests 'what is not said verbally is often said non-verbally'. The most effective communicators are those who are most aware of and able to manage their body language to maximise the effect of their message.

### Body posture

Different body postures send different messages. An open posture, where we face the person and maintain an open and upright stance, will usually send a positive message. It usually demonstrates a willingness to be vulnerable and exposed/open to the other person. A closed posture, on the other hand, where our arms are folded and we stand facing slightly away from the person, may reflect that we perceive the other person as a threat or are uncomfortable with them in some way (Boyes 2005: 24).

### Facial expression

The face is perhaps the centre of all non-verbal communication (Boyes 2005: 31). The facial expressions we use as we speak can contain a whole array of messages, which may be unconscious to us but noticeable to others. We have more than 90 muscles in the face, so it is unlikely that we will ever be able to control all of them. However, a wrinkle of the nose or a wink of an eye will certainly send a message to the recipient.

### Eyes and eye contact

It is a well-known expression that the eyes are the mirror to a person's soul. They certainly reveal our true feelings, showing us if someone is feeling sad even if they say they are feeling OK. The eyes give away our true emotions and most of us can 'sense' the reality of the other person, whether we trust these intuitive feelings or not!

A consideration when working with individuals with mental health conditions such as depression, bipolar disorder, schizophrenia or the misuse of substances may be the impact of their medication or the substance. These can give the eyes a glazed appearance or may reduce the facial expressions. Similarly, a person with Parkinson's disease may show a blank facial expression, but this does not mean that emotion is not present.

The amount of eye contact we give to another person may reflect how well we know them and how effectively we are relating to or communicating with them. However, as with all body language, eye contact is bound by specific rules, which include intimacy levels with the other person, age, gender and culture.

Staring is considered threatening, aggressive and rude across cultures. 'Giving someone the eyeball' while telling them off is a way of expressing power, rank and control. From a gender perspective, women usually use more eye contact than men. Boyes (2005: 34) suggests that women use eye contact to express involvement and interest, whereas men use it to indicate dominance and authority. Be aware that different cultures may construe eye contact differently, in some cultures, eye contact is sometimes viewed as a sexual invitation, while Muslim women usually avoid direct eye contact with men.

## Gestures

The movements of our hands, arms, legs, feet and head add to our communication. Consider raising the hand in front of you, with the palm facing towards the person. Without using words, this passes the message for the person to stop. Putting your thumbs up usually indicates that something is good, while a simple crossing of the fingers can indicate a wish for good luck. Stamping the foot or clenching the fists may indicate frustration, while moving the hands and lower arms a lot may reflect expressiveness or anxiety depending on one's perspective.

A further thought for consideration is that within different cultures, different gestures can have different meanings. In the UK, the thumb and forefinger touching is used to give an 'OK' signal, but in Brazil and the Middle East, this gesture has a totally different and much less polite meaning! In Italy and Greece, gesturing with hands during conversation reflects expression and passion. However, the quantity of gestures does not necessarily infer the emotion of the person. Some people gesticulate a lot as they speak to assist communication. Persons who are unable to communicate verbally (deaf or partial hearing) may use sign language (British Sign Language or variations) to communicate.

When listening to another person, being aware and sensitive to the gestures they use can assist with communication and can reflect attention. In some instances, raising awareness to these gestures (if appropriate) can be useful to explore what is truly being said. For example, in a coaching or counselling situation, a person who is telling you they think they can do something but shaking their head (unconsciously) from right to left (expressing 'no') may need to become aware of and explore their head shaking. The mismatch between their words and gestures may mean that at some level they do not believe in their ability. However, in some cultures (such as in Iran, Greece and Turkey) shaking the head can actually mean 'yes' (Boyes 2005: 28).

## Proximity/personal space

The closeness at which we stand to people will also affect communication. Each person will have their own comfort zone for intimacy with others. Usually, the closer we stand to someone, the more intimate the relationship or the happier we are to develop intimacy with that person. For example, cuddling and comforting someone is an expression of personal intimacy.

Some factors that influence our personal space boundaries include: physical stature, culture, topic of conversation, personality, gender, age, attraction and environment (e.g. our personal space boundaries are pushed in crowded places but this is accepted, whereas in a non-crowded environment, having someone stand very close to us may threaten our personal space and create feelings of discomfort).

A further consideration is that, while one person may want to develop intimacy, the other person may not. In professional environments, boundaries of role and ethical behaviour must be considered. Some vulnerable people can be less aware of boundaries and may behave more intimately and sometimes inappropriately for the situation. It is essential that the professional person be respectful but also assertive with these boundaries, to protect themselves (e.g. from any potential allegations of abuse) and the vulnerable person with whom they are working by mirroring appropriate boundaries assertively.

## SUMMARY

Listening involves not only listening to what a person is saying but how they say it – including their tone, emphasis and non-verbal communication. Focusing on all of this may be difficult at first but will soon become second nature and be a valuable asset in both professional and personal communication.

# POSITIONING

How we position ourselves during a consultation or assessment with a client is also important. Often the practitioner sits behind a desk, which proves a physical barrier, however, sitting too close may invade a client's personal space and cause them to feel uncomfortable, an equally difficult barrier. Both types of barriers can affect communication.

A useful acronym to use when working with clients is SOLER. This uses five basic elements to improve communication and listening skills:

S – face the client Squarely at a slight angle; this conveys involvement.

O – Open posture; this is seen as non-defensive and approachable.

L – Lean forward slightly; this shows interest.

E – maintain regular Eye contact, avoid looking away or focusing on notes.

R – Relax; a relaxed and comfortable manner communicates interest (adapted from Hunt and Hillsdon 2003: 49).

Always consider your position as this can reflect your interest in what is being said and towards the person. If we face them, we are demonstrating that they have our full attention. If we are side-on or facing away from them, it may reflect that we are distracted and no longer interested. However, avoid being directly in front of the client as this may appear confrontational or make them uncomfortable. Also consider matching or mirroring the client's posture to a degree, too much of a match may come across as intimidating while too opposite a posture can infer disinterest.

# ASSERTIVE COMMUNICATION

Being assertive requires expressing and acting on your own rights as a person while respecting the same rights in other people. Bayne et al (1998) indicate that every person's assertive rights include:

- To be treated with respect.
- To express their thoughts, feelings, values and opinions.
- To say 'no' without feeling guilty.
- To be successful.
- To make mistakes.
- To change their mind.
- To say they don't understand.
- To ask for what they want.
- To decide whether they are responsible for another person's problem or not.
- To choose not to assert themselves.

These rights apply equally to all people, and all communication should aim to maintain both respect of self and respect of the other person as well.

| Table 6.4 | Communication styles | | | |
|---|---|---|---|---|
| | **Assertive** | **Aggressive** | **Passive** | **Manipulative** |
| Position | I'm OK | You're not OK | I'm not OK | You're not OK, but I will let you think you are OK |
| Personal power | Shares power and willing to be vulnerable | Controls and dominates to have power | Helpless victim Gives power to others Uses guilt to control | Use deceit to gain control and power |
| How others feel | Respect Inspired Acceptance | Fear Humiliation Hurt | Guilty Lose respect Abused | Suspicious Confused Manipulated |
| Courage | Willing to deal with difficulty and pain | Attacks and blames others | Does not stand up for self | Feigns other emotions to cover own fear |
| Outcome | Peace of mind | Lonely and bitter | Martyrdom – life is hard | Loss of trust and respect |

Adapted from Phelps and Austin (1997). See also transactional analysis model in Chapter 3.

For example, expressing one's own opinion and values to discredit or hurt someone or without consideration to how your opinions affect the other person is not respectful or assertive. It can be seen as aggressive or manipulative communication, used to control, dominate or manipulate the other person. On the other hand, not expressing certain thoughts and our true feelings can be seen as passive communication, and may be a sign that we are giving our power away.

In reality, we communicate using a variety of these styles. The key is to be aware of which style we use predominately, in which situations and with which people. We can then choose to change the way we communicate to build the relationship.

When working towards assertive communication, it is essential to be realistic and to do your best, it may not always be perfect. Other people may not always respond assertively back, nor will they always appreciate your assertions. Sometimes being assertive will not achieve the desired outcome – getting what we want. In some situations and with some people it may not be easy to be assertive and in some situations we may choose not to be assertive. The positive thing is you can always try again (Phelps and Austin 1997).

A strategy for assertive communication is:

- Decide what you want to achieve from the communication and what needs to be expressed, with respect to all persons involved.
- Use 'I' statements ('I think …' or 'I feel …') to take ownership of thoughts and feelings.
- Support what you say with corresponding body language, voice tone and vocabulary.

- Stay focused and stick to the agenda, without being sidetracked or manipulated. You can deal with other issues later.
- Listen to the other person – they have a right to their point of view.
- Aim for a win-win cooperation.

For example, a client keeps missing appointments and always rings up to cancel at the last minute to say they cannot make it. They have missed the last three sessions and arrive back today. An assertive dialogue might begin with: 'I know that you sometimes find it a challenge to attend our sessions. I am concerned that if you keep missing days you will not experience the results that you said you wanted to achieve. I wonder if there is anything that you would like to change about the programme or if there is anything else getting in the way?' An aggressive approach would be: 'Look, if you keep missing sessions, you cannot expect to get the results you want!' A manipulative response could be a sarcastic 'How nice of you to turn up today', while a passive responder wouldn't bother saying anything, as they dislike any possible confrontation.

## USING COMMUNICATION TO HELP PEOPLE CHANGE

Throughout the day, our senses are subject to millions of different stimuli. The brain is not capable of processing all of this information and therefore a selection process occurs that determines which information the brain will process and give meaning, which will be stored away for future use and which will be discarded. The information that we chose to process will often be based on our values, what is important to us and our beliefs, opinions and perceptions of self and others. Every day we make assumptions or judgements based on the limited information that we chose to select. Often this information is selected to confirm our view or picture of the world. This can lead to self-limiting beliefs, for example, if a person is scared of exercising as a relative had a heart attack, they are likely to pay attention to stories where people have suffered adverse episodes while exercising, dismissing any stories where people have had improvements in health. Such self-limiting beliefs act as blinkers, narrowing our focus of information processed. When we decide to buy a new car, we suddenly see the make and model we would like on every street – this doesn't mean that suddenly there are more of that car on the road, but rather that we are noticing the car because it is important to us.

Language is another way in which we receive information and this, like all other stimuli, is open to interpretation. How often have you had a conversation with a friend or partner and think you have agreed a course of action, only to find out that their interpretation was completely different?

When working with clients, it is vital that the professional understands not only the words used by the client but their interpretation of those words. For example, a client comes to you and says they want to 'get fit', but what does the word 'fit' mean to them? An exercise professional may interpret fit to mean a balance of strength, suppleness, stamina, skill levels and speed; a health professional may focus on fit meaning lack of disease, while the individual may just want to be able to get up the stairs without getting out of breath. It is therefore vital that the practitioner understands exactly what the client means and has a clear understanding of their world, without allowing their own perceptions to influence their understanding. Once the professional has developed their understanding, they may then need to challenge the client's limiting beliefs, but in a manner that will support change and not create greater resistance. How do we do this? The first step is listening without prejudice and using questions to ensure that we have a very clear picture of the issue.

When clients speak, they often use very high level or vague language that makes it difficult to get a clear meaning and/or has been filtered to fit in with a person's beliefs. When speaking, clients may make statements that include generalisations, deletion or distortion of information and it is the professional's role to recover the missing parts of the picture and challenge the statement.

Generalisation applies when a person makes a statement that sounds like it applies to all situations but this is often based on little evidence. Examples include:

- Statements that contain the words 'can't', 'unable' or 'impossible', such as: 'It is impossible to work full time, have a family and find time to keep fit.' The questions the professional may ask include:
  - Says who?
  - What stops you from keeping fit?
  - What tells you that?
  - Do you know anyone that does?
  - How much time do you need to keep fit?
  - What if you could?
- Statements that include words such as 'need', 'must', 'should', 'have to', 'necessary', such as: 'I must get fit.' The questions to ask may include:
  - What do you mean by 'fit'?
  - Why must you get fit?

- What would happen if you didn't?
- What would happen if you did?
- Statements that include the word 'never', 'nobody', 'anyone' or 'everyone', such as: 'Nobody will support me in being active.' The questions to ask may include:
  - Nobody?
  - Is there one person who does/might?
  - Why do you think that?

Deletion applies when detail has been omitted from a statement, or selective attention is given to certain dimensions of the experience and excludes others. Examples include:

- Statements when information is missing, such as 'I feel stressed'. A professional's response question might be, 'About what exactly?'
- Statements where a hidden comparison is being made, such as 'My fitness is getting worse'. A response could be, 'Worse than what?'
- Statements where processes are being referred to as if they were fixed, such as, 'I'm a failure'. Responses could include:
  - At everything?
  - What exactly did you fail at?
  - Who says so?
- Statements where something is missing because they have not stated who or what is involved, such as 'I am uncomfortable'. Responses could include:
  - With what/whom?
  - When?
- Another example is when people make a general statement about their or other people's abilities, such as 'I'm not very good at this type of thing'. Here, questions to ask would be:
  - Compared to whom?

- Tell me more.
- What standard/who are you comparing yourself to?
- In what way?
- What specifically are you not good at?
- Similarly people can make statements where it is not clear what all the facts are, such as 'They annoy me'. Questions to ask here include:
  - What do they do that leads to you feeling annoyed?
  - How/when specifically?
  - Who are they?

Distortion applies when we add our own inference to something, i.e. if x happens, it means y. Examples include:

- A statement that implies that there is a cause and effect, such as 'My boss makes me stressed'. Responses could be:
  - What specifically are they doing to make you feel stress?
  - What is your boss doing when you choose to feel stressed?
- A statement that implies the professional can mind-read, such as 'I know you don't understand'. Questions to ask here include:
  - How do you know?
  - What tells you that?
- A statement that implies that one thing is automatically related to something else, such as 'My husband does not love me because I am fat'. Responses could include:
  - In what way do you think that you being fat means he does not love you?
  - In what ways does he show you he loves you?

Further examples of different linguistic patterns can be found in *The Structure of Magic* by Bandler and Grinder (1975).

The use of such statements often hides a deeper meaning and shines a light on some of the beliefs that may limit choice as clients often use negative statements based on past experience and apply them to the present, for example:

- I can't lose weight
- I can't walk for more than 15 minutes
- I am not flexible.

It is important that the professional challenge these beliefs as they will have an impact on the client's ability to change behaviour as clients will continue to collect information and behave in manner that confirms their beliefs. The use of appropriate questions, as highlighted above, can assist in challenging these beliefs. This can be strengthened if the professional can create experiences in which the client succeeds and also provide feedback on the progress the client has made and the skills and abilities they have.

# COMMUNICATION AND SENSORY IMPAIRMENT

A chapter on communication would not be complete without a few words on communicating with individuals with sensory impairments.

## HEARING IMPAIRMENT

According to recent health statistics (HSE 2008) more than 15 per cent of adults report hearing difficulties, rising to around one third of adults aged 65 years and above.

An individual with hearing problems may experience the following issues:

- Being unable to distinguish the speech of other people clearly.
- A reduced ability to hear a range of sounds. Higher pitched voices and soft or weak tones may cause particular problems.
- Loud noise or sounds, e.g. heavy bass beats in music.
- Mishearing similar sounding words, e.g. hall, ball, tall, etc.
- Problems with background noises or simultaneous conversations.
- Tinnitus (ringing in the ears).

In addition, some adults with severe or profound deafness may have a speech impairment, so always ask if you are unsure what has been said and, in cases where you still do not understand after repetition, ask for it to be written down.

Many older adults often prefer to hide their hearing issues or are adept at lip-reading, so you need to look for signs of difficulty, such as the client:

- Looking puzzled.
- Straining to hear.
- Asking for a repetition of what was said.
- Misunderstanding or ignoring what is said.

Ensure that you include a range of communication styles in your sessions and assessments. Consider using large visual cues, speaking when facing the person, using a normal speed of speech and not obstructing the mouth when speaking, these all help to make communication clear. It is also important to avoid speaking away from the person or chewing gum as these may make your speech harder to understand. During classes where music is used, ask if the volume is comfortable and let the participants choose where they stand; being too close to a speaker may cause discomfort.

Always ask which is the preferred method of contact – communicating by text or email may be preferred to telephone calls, while Typetalk may be preferred when using the telephone.

British Sign Language (BSL) is the first language for more than 50,000 people in the UK, so it may be worth doing a BSL course if you are working with adults who are deaf or hearing impaired on a regular basis. Contact Action on Hearing Loss (formerly the RNID) for further details (www.actiononhearingloss.org.uk).

## Lip-reading

Lip-reading is often used by individuals with poor or no hearing, but it is a complex and tiring skill and often only the key words are picked up, which means instructions may need to be clarified or written down.

When communicating with an individual with any form of hearing impairment or who lip-reads, bear the following in mind:

- Stand in front of the person so they can see your face clearly.
- Speak in a normal way, don't speed up or slow down or try to exaggerate your speech patterns as this is confusing for the individual.
- If they have an interpreter, allow time for the message to be conveyed. And ALWAYS talk to the person not the interpreter.
- Keep your hair, hands or pens away from your mouth.
- Don't chew gum!
- Remember that lip-readers are often adept at reading what you are saying from a distance so be careful about any comments you make to others.

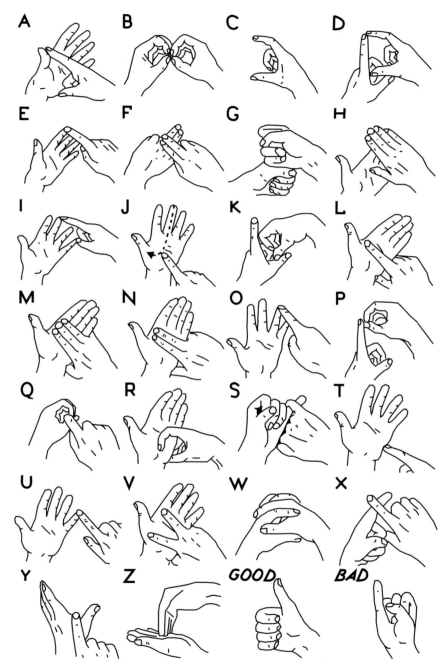

**Figure 6.3** BSL alphabet

## Visual impairment

Communicating with adults with visual impairments may require careful planning. It is estimated that around 6 per cent of all adults have a visual impairment, rising to one in five people aged 75 years or above. Not all adults wear the correct prescription glasses, if they wear them at all, so it may not be obvious at first.

Make sure any forms, information or cards are available in a large font and make visual and verbal demonstrations clear. Allow plenty of time for reading and completing forms (and be aware that a person may say they have not got their glasses with them to cover up being unable to read).

If someone is completely blind, ask them how you can help with communication or getting around, it is much better asking than to try and figure it out, which can lead to misunderstanding and embarrassment on all sides.

When working with either visual or hearing impaired clients, allow time for them to watch or listen to instructions and demonstrations, give plenty of 'rehearsal' time and use a variety of different methods of communication to enhance the experience for all. For example, podcasts or recorded instructions and programmes may be useful for those with an mp3 player and Braille formats may need to be available for those who read in this way.

For information on working with blind and visually impaired individuals, contact the Royal National Institute of Blind People (www.rnib.org.uk).

## Intellectual disabilities

Working with individuals who have a learning disability, Down's syndrome or a cognitive impairment (collectively known as intellectual disabilities) presents different challenges to communication. However, positive lifestyle changes are equally important for this population group, so instructors may work with individuals with mild to moderate intellectual disabilities. If there is any uncertainty about the level of understanding, it is recommended that a helper is present to aid communication. However, if a helper is present, it is important to direct questions and answers to the client, not the helper.

Makaton is a universal form of sign language used in learning disabilities and it is worth learning a few signs to help with communication if you are working with this client group on a regular basis (see Figure 6.4).

## SUMMARY

Every area of life is affected by communication. A lack of communication or communication of poor quality can lead to misunderstanding and isolation, while being bombarded by stimuli can create overload and stress in the mind. Finding a balance between the two is important, while being able to adapt personal communication to suit the client or person you are with is an important skill that will help with all areas of life. The focus is often on one aspect of communication, yet the three areas outlined above – verbal, para-verbal and non-verbal – form a powerful combination and all need to be 'read' or listened to if the underlying message is to be understood. Consider the person who asks their partner what the matter is and receives the word 'nothing' in response. It would be easy to assume that nothing is indeed wrong. However, if the tone is flat and the partner crossed their arms and purses their lips while saying it, then the meaning is almost certainly 'something' and should be explored!

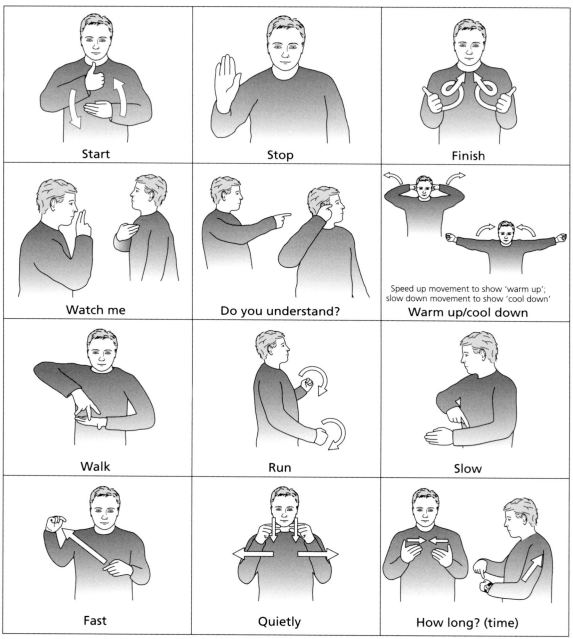

**Figure 6.4** Makaton signs

adapted from S. Wicebloom, *Training Disabled People*, page 103.

## KEY POINTS

- The communication process has three key aims:
  - To build rapport.
  - To understand the client's perspective or map of the world.
  - To determine the client's readiness to change or motivations to change.
- To do this the practitioner needs to consider their own and their client's communication, including:
  - What they are saying – verbal.
  - How they are saying it – para-verbal.
  - What their body is saying – non-verbal.
- Practising good communication skills in everyday life will help to improve skills in professional life and help clients in the process of change.

And remember, we all get it wrong sometimes!

# TOOLS AND STRATEGIES TO HELP BEHAVIOURAL CHANGE

7

Successful and permanent change is the goal of any practitioner working with clients in the health-related fitness environment. We have considered the models, theories and skills used in behaviour change and will now look at a range of tools to assist the process of change. As previously discussed, theories and models tend not to fit the individual client, so using communication – as outlined in Chapter 6 – in combination with the tools and strategies discussed below is important in finding a client-centred solution to change. Remember, however, that these may not provide a perfect fit for the client either. Indeed the practitioner can – and should – adapt, amend or devise new strategies that they feel will provide a better approach for the client.

The aims of this chapter are:

- To review the role of the practitioner.
- To review the use of goal-setting in behaviour change.
- To identify different types of goal-setting approaches.
- To discuss a range of motivational tools and strategies that can be used in behaviour change including:
  - Visualisation

- Decisional balance
- WRECK
- Managing lapses
- Abstinence of violation effect

## THE ROLE OF THE PRACTITIONER

The practitioner, whether a fitness instructor, exercise referral specialist or sports coach, has a significant role in facilitating change. It is therefore important to understand not only the elements of the role but also the limits and boundaries that need to be in place.

### INCREASING SELF-EFFICACY

The evidence has highlighted the importance of self-efficacy in effective behaviour change. It is important that the professional helps to support increases in self-efficacy. Here are some of the things the professional can do:

- Support the client in setting stretching but achievable goals.
- Provide the client with feedback on their progress towards goals and indicate where effective action has been taken. The professional

has an important role in providing positive feedback and ensuring that the client does not miss any actions they have carried out that will move them closer to their goals and reinforce this effective behaviour.

- Providing examples of models/peers who exhibit the behaviour so that they can see that it is possible.
- Persuading the client that they have the ability to be active and get fitter.
- Highlighting the benefits of the behaviour.

## TEACH SELF-MONITORING

- Teach the client how to monitor their performance – this could take the form of teaching them how to use perceived exertion to be able to monitor their sessions. This will put them in control and enable them to monitor how their fitness improves.
- The practitioner can also use tools such as diaries to help clients identify the triggers or cues for unhealthy behaviour and any barriers to improving behaviour.

## FEEDBACK AND REINFORCEMENT

- The practitioner's role is to provide positive feedback to the client, shining a light on positive behaviour and encouraging best practice.
- The practitioner also has a role in highlighting to the client progress using logs or charts alongside positive communication. They also need to teach the client how to self-monitor (see above).

## FOLLOW-UP SUPPORT

Research evidence highlights the importance of frequent follow up to help consolidate change (Artinian et al 2010). This can take the format of direct contact or contact by phone or email. The exact amount of contact is not clear from the evidence but it is suggested that once the intervention has ended that contact should be once every three months for the first year and then every six months thereafter.

## CREATING SOCIAL SUPPORT

Social support is a key element in successful change. Some clients may not have support at home for being active and therefore would benefit from support from a group of peers. This is where creating group sessions can be beneficial so consider the practicalities of this when starting to work with clients.

## SKILL DEVELOPMENT AND RELAPSE PREVENTION

A further role of the practitioner is to ensure that the client has the appropriate skills to maintain change, and undertake long-term participation in physical activity. In addition to learning practical skills such as weight training, how to monitor training or how to build activity into daily life, it is also important that the professional looks at helping clients develop strategies regarding how to deal with potential trigger points that could lead to lapse, and strategies for what to do when clients do lapse.

## WHEN TO USE TOOLS

There is no guide setting out the best time to use each tool. The key is to get to know your client and work with them to decide which tool is appropriate in which stage. Some may work well in one stage but not in others, while some may not work at all! It is all about working in a client-centred way to assist them in finding out what is the best fit for them.

Some clients thrive on fixed SMART goals, while others find they need more flexible targets and aims. Some will need regular reviews while others may prefer to just get on with it without help. Whatever tool you use, the key is to design and apply it in a way that the client feels comfortable with.

It would be useful for the practitioner to try each of the following tools themselves before using them with others to gain experience of any advantages and disadvantages and identify ways they may be used helpfully.

## GOAL-SETTING

Alice: Could you tell me please, which way I ought to go?

Cheshire Cat: That depends a great deal upon where you want to go.

Alice: I don't know.

Cheshire Cat: Then it really doesn't matter which way you go, does it?
> From *Alice in Wonderland* by Lewis Carroll.

Setting appropriate goals is a useful tool for successful change. If goals are set too low or are too easy, then people don't bother to work towards them. Alternatively, setting goals too high, or making them too specific or too vague, means that the opportunity for 'failure' is high. Goals should be designed not just as something to aim towards but also to give a clear vision of the outcome.

Goal-setting is a simple technique that is used to strengthen an individual's motivation when changing behaviours. It involves using a range of person-centred communication skills (as described in the previous chapters) to gather information about the client to ascertain their true motivations or wants. This process can be very effective when used properly, however, it is all too often practised inefficiently, which can hinder motivation and progress instead of helping it.

For goal-setting to be motivational, what an individual really wants to achieve must be discovered. Often there is a focus on what an instructor (or indeed the client) thinks the client 'needs' or 'should' want, and this type of extrinsic goal-setting can make the client feel that they have not been listened to, as well as making resulting goals insufficiently attractive or important. Only goals that are intrinsic to an individual, that have a value for them, are likely to encourage change.

Goal-setting can be used at any stage in the process of change. It can help to prepare for change, to move towards change, to measure progress and anticipate any setbacks along the way and to maintain change with ongoing new goals. It can also be simple or complex, so to illustrate the process, let's imagine we are going by car to a wedding that starts at 1pm. The wedding is in a town some distance away and it is the first time we have ever been there.

The first things we need to consider are:

- Where are we going? Lonchester
- How far is it? 200 miles
- How long will it take? 3.5 hours according to a route planner
- What time do we need to get there? 12.45pm
- Simple goal: Leave home at 9.15am to get to Lonchester at 12.45pm.

As long as the travelling conditions are good, we can assume that we will reach our destination on time. However, there may be obstacles along the way that we need to consider or we could find ourselves missing the 'I do' because we didn't!

Additional considerations include:

- What might happen during the journey that may cause delays? For example, road works, traffic jams, weather conditions, diversions, breakdown, etc.

We need to build in some time to allow for any of these problems so we need to revise our setting-off time by adding extra 30 minutes to the journey, just in case. So now our adapted goal is to leave home at 8.45am to get to Lonchester by 12.45pm.

- But we should stop for a break. That can add 15 minutes or so.

So our revised goal is now to leave home at 8.30am to get to Lonchester by 12.45pm. It is also sensible to consider other planning and pre-travel checks to make sure that any other potential problems are unlikely to delay us further.

- Do I have enough petrol in the tank? Do I know where I can fill up on the way?
- Have I got water, a snack and my wallet?
- Is my mobile phone charged?
- Is there enough oil in the car?
- Are the tyres inflated properly?
- Do I need to top up the water in the washer system?
- Are all the lights working properly?
- Is my insurance/tax/MOT up to date?

- Have I got breakdown cover? What exactly does it cover?

And finally:

- Should I get that funny knocking sound investigated? (Note: YES!)

Therefore, considering everything, our final goal is to leave home at 8.30 to get to Lonchester by 12.45pm.

This might seem like a lot of planning just to arrive on time, or possibly early, but you probably do this every day for one reason or another; it might be a journey, going on holiday or just going shopping but we all plan towards the end goal – whatever it is.

So, what it the moral of this story? Think about where your client is now, think about where they want to be and then take into account any problems, obstacles or events that may occur. As the old saying goes 'fail to prepare, prepare to fail.'

## GOAL MOTIVATION

People may be motivated to achieve their outcome goal for many different reasons – they may be moving towards pleasure or away from pain, their goal may be focused on elimination (giving something up) or achievement (gaining something) giving their goal a positive or negative bias.

| Pain | Pleasure |
|------|----------|
| Negative bias | Positive bias |
| Elimination | Achievement |
| Cessation | Gain |

**Figure 7.1** Pleasure or pain as motivation

| Table 7.1 | Rewording task | |
|---|---|---|
| Task: The following goals are based on moving away from pain; reword them in positive terms, without losing the essence of the goal – if you can. | | |
| 1 | I will stop smoking | 1 |
| 2 | I will stop eating crisps | 2 |
| 3 | I will stop letting people bully me | 3 |
| 4 | I will give up drinking alcohol | 4 |
| 5 | I will lose weight so people don't judge me | 5 |

Essentially, pleasure vs. pain and achievement vs. elimination are similar in aspect. The person is either moving towards a pleasurable outcome such as wearing a smaller dress size or having better control of their diabetes, or they may be moving away from a painful situation, such as being stigmatised because of their size or having a restricted lifestyle due to diabetic complications. Whatever the situation, be guided by the client and their motivations as this is all about them.

When setting goals, regardless of the motivation, it is good to have a positive outcome, a sense of gaining something. Goals that are focused on 'giving up', 'losing', 'I will no longer …' imply loss or deprivation of some kind and may feel less motivational while phrases such as 'I will be …', I will gain …' imply benefits gained, which is more likely to motivate someone. This may be hard to do if the motivation is to move away from pain, however, the right wording of the goal can make a big difference to how it is perceived.

## KEY CONSIDERATIONS

The skill of goal-setting is to make it relevant to the client and to choose something that excites them, which will help motivation. A goal of giving up chocolate will be hard to stick to for someone who likes chocolate, but a goal of allowing a small amount of chocolate once a day is more likely to be achieved, as it does not involve 'deprivation'.

When helping clients set their goals remember the following considerations:

1 Make goals specific in terms of their outcomes – a vague goal such as 'I am going to lose a bit of weight' is unlikely to be motivating, and the client will not know when they have achieved it.

2 Don't make the goal too far in the future. Something that is too far in the future may seem unobtainable, so set shorter-term goals of a maximum of a few months.

3 Make them realistic but stretching – this is the art of goal-setting. Goals need to be achievable but also need to give the person a sense of achievement to be both motivating and to support increases in self-efficacy.

4 Focus on the behaviour and how the person is going to reach the outcome. Sometimes people set goals that are outside their control, for example, focusing on a health outcome such as being able to reduce their medication. While this may be a by-product of the behaviour, the goals should focus on the behaviour itself, e.g. I am going to walk three times a week.

5  The client should be able to track that they are achieving their goal, getting regular feedback on progress. This could be as simple as seeing that a pair of trousers is fitting them better or as complex as a higher score on the bleep test.

Goals should be set by the client. While there is evidence that both professional- and client-led goal setting can be successful, a number of methods such as motivational interviewing highlight the importance of the client's goals being developed by the client, with the professional's role being to help shape these goals to meet the above rules. For example:

- I will lose three stone in six months:
  - I will do this by giving up chocolate and treats.
- I will be one dress size smaller in six months:
  - I will do this by making one small change to my diet each week.
  - I will go for a walk for at least 20 minutes, three times a week.
  - I will eat smaller portions of food at mealtimes.
  - I will eat at least one more piece of fruit each day.

This is essentially the same outcome goal, yet the second set is positively phrased giving it a sense of 'gain' and avoiding a sense of deprivation which is likely to make it more motivational.

## DIFFERENT TYPES OF GOAL

In general, goals fall into two types, *outcome* and *process*. An outcome goal is the ultimate destination and there are only two possible results, success or failure. This can be demotivating, as outcome goals tend to be large or complex and do not allow for even a slight margin of error. While this may work if you are an athlete or sportsperson training for a big event, it is not a particularly person-centred way of working. Outcome goals also tend to be longer-term and this can seem a long way off, and less easy to visualise when starting out. When we start a large task or project, it is usual to break it into smaller steps and complete these one at a time to make the final target seem less daunting.

These smaller steps are known as process goals or targets that work towards the outcome goal in smaller chunks. As they are smaller, they are more manageable and can be less rigid, making them more likely to be achieved, which will improve motivation and self-efficacy on the path towards the ultimate outcome goal. Process goals can also be viewed as short-term, medium-term and long-term, depending on the scale or timeframe of the outcome goal.

When making changes to any element of lifestyle it may be better to start with process goals and keep the final outcome as a more distant aim. Figure 7.2 gives examples of each type with a clear outcome goal followed by smaller steps, or process goals that will help to achieve this.

## OUTCOME GOALS AND SMART GOAL-SETTING

Goal-setting comes in many forms and a common method used is known as SMART. This uses a simple process (that often becomes unnecessarily complicated and off-putting), that takes idealistic dreams and makes them achievable goals. There are many variations of this form of goal-setting

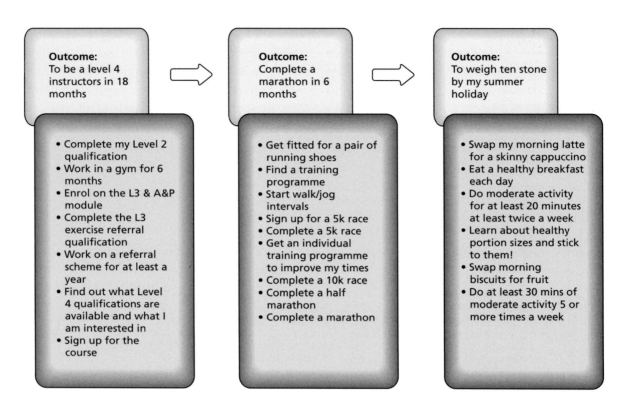

**Outcome:**
To be a level 4 instructors in 18 months

- Complete my Level 2 qualification
- Work in a gym for 6 months
- Enrol on the L3 & A&P module
- Complete the L3 exercise referral qualification
- Work on a referral scheme for at least a year
- Find out what Level 4 qualifications are available and what I am interested in
- Sign up for the course

**Outcome:**
Complete a marathon in 6 months

- Get fitted for a pair of running shoes
- Find a training programme
- Start walk/jog intervals
- Sign up for a 5k race
- Complete a 5k race
- Get an individual training programme to improve my times
- Complete a 10k race
- Complete a half marathon
- Complete a marathon

**Outcome:**
To weigh ten stone by my summer holiday

- Swap my morning latte for a skinny cappuccino
- Eat a healthy breakfast each day
- Do moderate activity for at least 20 minutes at least twice a week
- Learn about healthy portion sizes and stick to them!
- Swap morning biscuits for fruit
- Do at least 30 mins of moderate activity 5 or more times a week

**Figure 7.2** Outcome and process goals

and the letters can stand for anything that is personal to the individual. However, the following are commonly used:

- S = Specific
- M = Measurable
- A = Achievable
- R = Relevant (or Realistic)
- T = Time framed

SMART can be made SMARTER by adding E and R.

- E = Exciting/Evaluated: If the goal is exciting, it is more likely to be motivational and progress should be evaluated regularly so that adjustments can be made if necessary.
- R = Recorded/Rewarded: Recording the goal in a diary, on paper or as a screensaver makes it real and planning rewards helps with motivation.

Each element of SMART needs to answer some basic questions to ensure the goal is relevant, tangible and real to the client.

**Specific**

- What is the specific goal the client wants to achieve?
- Why is this goal important to the client, what are the benefits, what will they gain?
- The more specific the goal is, the easier it is to focus on it and monitor progress

**Measurable**

- Against what criteria will the goal be measured?
- How will you know when the goal is achieved?
- Goals that are not measurable are likely to be vague and hard to assess

**Achievable**

- Does the client have the ability and attitude to achieve the goal?
- Does the client have the necessary support or resources?
- A client who wants to lose weight needs to be in an environment where healthy eating is possible, being around others who overeat or overconsume unhealthy food makes it much harder to succeed

**Relevant**

- Is the goal relevant to the client, how will they 'use' it?
- Unrealistic goals such as never eating chocolate again have little chance of success if it is something the client enjoys – better to reduce the amount than ban it!

**Time framed**

- Is there a specific time frame for the goal?
- Is the time frame appropriate for achieving the goal?
- An appropriate time frame creates a sense of urgency and importance which will help with motivation

**Exciting**

- Is the client excited by the goal?
- Can they visualise themselves reaching the goal?
- Goals that excite the client and that they can visualise themselves achieving are more likely to succeed

**Recorded and rewarded**

- Has the client written the goal down?
- Have they planned a reward for achieving the goal?
- Writing goals down and looking at them keeps them in our minds and having a reward planned gives the process a value

**Figure 7.3** SMARTER goals

It may be helpful to also consider the S as Simple – keep the wording of the actual goal simple, short and sweet, avoiding overlong and complicated sentences as these may be confusing or disguise the actual goal. SMART goals make good targets or outcomes, while the actual means will be more suitable as process goals and are more likely to focus on behaviour. Consider the difference between:

- Goal A: I will shave ten minutes off my marathon time in six months.
- Goal B: I will increase the amount of running I do each week and go to the gym three times a week so I improve my fitness and can run my next marathon in six months' time ten minutes faster.

The first sentence is an excellent SMART goal; it could be written in large letters on a piece of paper and stuck on the fridge as a constant reminder. The second is really a series of process statements and would be more effective if written as such. A more effective way of setting out the goal would be:

- My goal is to shave ten minutes off my marathon time in six months.
  To do this I will:
  - Gradually increase my running time each week.
  - Attend the gym regularly to improve my muscular fitness to help with running endurance.
  - Research a healthy eating plan for running and follow it.

To use SMART goal-setting as an effective motivational tool we need to find out what a person wants, what their driving force is and what resources they have. Often clients will come to you with very vague ideas of what they want to achieve, so as the practitioner you must use communication skills to gain a more precise idea of what the person wants in order to construct their goal. These are examples of common statements that need to be turned into goals.

- I want to lose weight.
- I want be a bit fitter.
- I want to get rid of my diabetes.

'I want to lose weight' is very vague, so start by asking how much weight they want to lose. By when? Often this will be an unrealistic amount that may be the very long-term ideal but which needs breaking down into smaller amounts to make it both achievable and realistic. For example, 'I weigh 250 pounds now and want to weigh 150 pounds in six months'. This is unrealistic for health reasons and the slow and sensible weight loss of one to two pounds a week will not only feel like very small amounts, but will also not get them to their dream – so they will 'fail'. The instructor needs to work with them to break their overall goal down into manageable short-term goals that are both realistic and achievable. Setting a goal of losing four pounds in the first month is achievable and will promote a sense of achievement when it is reached. Reassessing the weight loss and setting a new target for the next month will help promote sensible weight loss that is likely to be sustained. By setting these smaller, shorter goals it keeps the client motivated and when they get to 170 pounds, they may feel that is actually a good weight for them and stick there. (NB: Goals based on the fit of clothes or dress sizes may be more useful than weight loss as weight can fluctuate daily, weekly, monthly and, as muscle weighs more than fat, tissue weight can actually increase even though the client is getting smaller!)

'I want be a bit fitter' is similarly vague, so a good strategy is to ask the person what they will be able to do when they are fitter that they can't do now. They may currently get out of breath when climbing stairs or be unable to keep up with a softball game at work, so these more specific ideas can be used as the starting point for goal-setting.

'I want to get rid of my diabetes' is unrealistic, as it may not be medically possible to 'get rid' of their condition. However, setting a more realistic target of managing blood glucose levels is achievable and may reduce the impact of diabetes in the longer term.

## PROCESS GOALS: P4 – THE POWER OF 4

Process goals should be positive, palatable, possible and personal, starting with small, achievable steps.

Positive: Use goals that indicate a gain for the person and avoid phrases such as 'lose', 'give up', 'won't', etc. as these imply denial or loss.

Palatable: Goals need to be appealing to the person. If they are unpalatable, they are unlikely to be successful as no one really wants to work towards something in which they are not interested.

Possible: Goals must be realistic or they have no chance!

Personal: The goal must be personal to the individual, not a generic goal. For example, 'I will be one dress size smaller in eight weeks' is much more personal than 'as a family, we will lose two stone between us'.

## GOAL-SETTING WITH NEUROLINGUISTIC PROGRAMMING

In NLP, the term 'well-informed outcome' can be used to inform the development of effective goals. In addition to the considerations stated above, NLP practice encourages the client to 'visualise' and describe the outcome in great detail, as well as ensuring the selected goal fits with the values of the client, and is therefore more likely to be achieved. The following list of questions provides examples of those that the practitioner may wish to use when goal-setting (adapted from Carroll 2007).

- Positively stated – what the person wants, e.g. 'I want to be able to …'
- When, where and with who do you want it? – giving a clear picture of the goal and the timescales.
- Where are you now? – this gets the client to start thinking about what they will need to do to achieve the goal.
- What will you be seeing, hearing and feeling when you get it? – this gives the client a clear picture of what the goal will look like.
- What will you be able to do after you get it? – this will help identify some of the motivating factors.
- Who is this for? – checking that it is client-centred, and they are not doing it because someone else has told them to.
- What resources are needed? Have you ever done anything like this before? Do you know anyone who has? – identifying previous experience or potential role models that may help.
- What will happen if you get it? What won't happen if you get it? What will happen if you don't get it? What won't happen if you don't get it? – this can help you see how motivated/

committed the client is and what is at the centre of them wanting to achieved the goal. The motivation to get fit may be driven by a number of reasons ranging from wanting to improve health to being more attractive.

## VISUALISING GOALS

Practising visualising goals is a useful tool, because if the individual can visualise the outcome it makes it much more real and attainable and will create greater motivation. For example, if the goal is to lose weight it can help for the client to create a picture of the successful outcome by asking questions such as:

- How will you look?
- What clothes will you be wearing?
- What colours will you wear?
- How will you be feeling about yourself?
- Where will you be (what place)?
- What will you be doing?
- What will you be saying?
- What will your best friends be saying?

These are just some of the qualities of the image the client may see, and that they can change or leave the same. They can change the qualities of the image, by making the sounds louder or the colours brighter or focusing on specific details. By doing this, the image becomes amplified and thus more real and desirable.

## A NOTE OF CAUTION

Bear in mind that goals often involve giving up or cutting down on something that gives the person pleasure – for example, giving up chocolate, alcohol or lounging in front of the television can lead to feelings of deprivation and a sense of unfairness. Therefore, all goals should have some leeway for off days or include a couple of treats as standard. Often being 'allowed' to have a glass of wine with dinner results in the individual choosing not to, and that element of personal choice is important in adherence to change.

## KEY GOAL-SETTING TIPS:

- Positivity: Make goals positive to foster a sense of achievement and gain.
- Precision: Precise goals mean you know how you are doing and make it easy to know when you reach your goal.
- Prioritise: If you have several things you want to achieve, give priority to the one that means the most or that you feel better equipped to achieve.
- Progress: Set small, incremental process goals that give you a sense of control and keep you motivated towards the bigger outcome goal.
- Planning: Make allowances for obstacles or setbacks that may arise. If you are prepared for lapses, they are less likely to become relapses.
- Pragmatic: Be realistic about your ability to achieve a goal. It may be something you want and can do, however, you may not have the time or resources to achieve it. If this is the case, be realistic and adapt or change the goal.
- Postpone: If circumstances or priorities change, then postpone your goal for a while. Postponing is a more positive and realistic move than keeping going when 'failure' is inevitable.
- Prizes: Having a reward or prize in mind when you have achieved your goal is important – you deserve it after all the effort!

## Table 7.2  SMART goal task

Task

Consider the following goals, are they SMART? If not, identify ways to make them SMARTER and set some initial process goals.

| Client and goal | Bob wants to lose five stone in six months. He is currently 17.5 stone/110kg and is 5'8"/173cm. He is going to go to the gym every day for an hour, even though he doesn't like it, but he doesn't want to change his eating patterns. |
| --- | --- |
| Is this realistic? | |
| What goal would you set? | |
| What process goals would be appropriate? | • <br> • <br> • |
| Client and goal | Janet is doing the Three Peaks Challenge in two months. She walks to work every day, which is one mile and takes her 20 minutes. She thinks that if she walks home every day as well, this will be enough to get her fit for the challenge. |
| Is this realistic? | |
| What goal would you set? | |
| What process goals would be appropriate? | • <br> • <br> • |
| Client and goal | Hugh plays rugby every couple of weeks and has signed up for a half triathlon in three months. He says his once-a-week rugby training and a quick swim after work on Mondays will get him fit for this. |
| Is this realistic? | |
| What goal would you set? | |
| What process goals would be appropriate? | • <br> • <br> • |
| Client and goal | Colin has entered a bodybuilding competition in three months. He is going to train every day with his friends and use protein shakes to help him bulk up. He is a typical ectomorph and is 6'3"/191cm in height and just under 13 stone/82kg. |
| Is this realistic? | |
| What goal would you set? | |
| What process goals would be appropriate? | • <br> • <br> • |

## A cautionary tale: Sarah and the periodic table

A couple of years back Sarah decided that her New Year resolution would be to memorise the periodic table of the elements by Easter.

Why? Because she had always wanted to.

This goal was specific, measurable, achievable, realistic and timed so all the elements (ha, ha) were in place.

Did she succeed?

No.

Why not? Mainly because it had absolutely no relevance to her life or work and therefore was not important, so she kept putting it off when other more urgent things cropped up.

Having realised in March that it was not going to happen, Sarah officially *unset* the goal and went out and bought a mug with the periodic table on it!

The moral of the story?

However SMART a goal is, it may still not be right for you at the time or may become less important or practical over time. Goals can be changed, unset or amended at any time without 'failing'; in fact trying to stick to a redundant goal because you feel you have to is pointless and almost certainly doomed to failure.

Relevance, importance and desire are key motivational factors in goals, without these elements, they are much less likely to be successful.

P.S. Her next goal is to learn the NATO alphabet (sierra, alpha, romeo, alpha, hotel – what does that spell?)

# CONSCIOUS CHANGE

A useful strategy in promoting and maintaining change is to make the individual conscious of their ability to take control. This may require some help in the early stages, when the person can feel overwhelmed by the thought of changing behaviour and suffer from low self-esteem, however, if taken in slow steps, it will provide a supportive aid to change.

## STEPS TO CONSCIOUS CHANGE
### Step 1: Identify

The individual can use food diaries to monitor what, when and why they eat. Initially this should be an impartial log of food intake and feelings, which is then examined to see if any patterns occur. This must be an honest exercise to be useful, so it is important that the individual is in control and the role of the instructor should be that of a guide and not an interpreter.

### Step 2: Decide

The next step is to decide to make some changes in food habits. Focus on one or two smaller and easier changes initially to promote self-confidence when they are achieved. Set goals for these changes and make them positive and exciting.

### Step 3: Reward

When the first two changes have been successfully adopted and maintained for a while, identify a suitable reward to mark the achievement. This cycle can be repeated many times with a view to tackling behaviour patterns in small manageable stages, which is likely to be more successful than trying to change everything all at once.

## Step 4: Do more

As self-efficacy grows, it is time to make new changes and perhaps look at introducing activity into everyday life. As before, start with small achievable targets such as walking for an extra ten minutes a day or going for a swim once a week and building up gradually.

## DECISIONAL BALANCE/ PROS AND CONS

Decisional balance is a useful tool to use with clients who are aware of a need to change but are ambivalent about change. It can help to identify the reasons for making certain changes and the reasons for not making certain changes.

Decisional balance is ideally used in the contemplation stage, as it can help set out in black and white the benefits of adopting healthier lifestyle behaviours. The client identifies a concern and fills in the advantages and disadvantages of changing and of staying as they are. Ideally, they will end up with lots of reasons to change and not many reasons to stay as they are. Once completed, you may need to give them time to think about it and consider their options instead of jumping in with immediate solutions.

A word of caution, using the disadvantages or negative element of decisional balance can lead to sustain talk and the client may find reasons not to change. Keeping the focus on the advantages and gains may lead to more change talk.

How to create decisional balance sheets:

1  Draw four boxes – see Figure 7.4.
2  Write the following questions in each box:
   • What are the advantages of making changes?
   • What are the advantages of NOT making changes?
   • What are the disadvantages of making changes?
   • What are the disadvantages of NOT making changes?
3  Get the client to answer the questions.

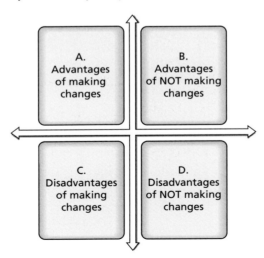

**Figure 7.4** Decisional balance sheet

4　Explore the responses as these offer a starting point to explore the potential motivations and barriers and also change and sustain talk.

Figure 7.5 is an example of a completed decisional balance sheet.

**Figure 7.5** Example completed decisional balance sheet

A more detailed example of a decisional balance sheet is included below.

| Table 7.3 | Decisional balance worksheet |
|---|---|
| **The behaviour or habit I want to change is:** | |
| ♂ The advantages of changing | ♀ The disadvantages of changing |
| | |
| If you can think of more disadvantages than advantages of changing, look at the disadvantages and identify ways to reduce them. | |
| Disadvantages of changing behaviour | Ways of reducing disadvantages |
| | |
| ♂ The advantages of NOT changing | ♀ The disadvantages of NOT changing |
| | |
| If you can think of more advantages than disadvantages of not changing, it may be time to re-evaluate your goal and consider a different one. | |

# LAPSE MANAGEMENT

Relapse and returning to old behaviours is always a risk for anyone making efforts to change. Relapse can destroy the will of those who start with the highest aspirations and the best of intentions. It can trigger feelings of failure and push the person to return to their old behaviour, and can leave them feeling that they are incompetent (a failure).

Strategies for promoting adherence and preventing relapse may include:

- Using appropriate goals and targets that are personal and relevant.
- Planning for high-risk situations.
- Making small changes gradually to minimise lapses.

- Reinforcing the positive benefits from change.
- Rewarding success with appropriate 'treats'.
- Viewing lapses as normal and temporary.
- Seeking positive support from friends and family.

Use these techniques in the early stages of each phase of change, and apply to the situations where the person will be most at risk of relapsing.

Identify any high-risk situations and typical responses. Once the high-risk situation has been identified, strategies can be put in place to either prevent (proactive) or manage (reactive) the situation.

| Table 7.3 | Managing risk | |
|---|---|---|
| **High-risk situations** | | |
| **Hazard** | | **Control strategy** |
| Situations associated with overeating such as coffee and biscuits, dinner out. | ⇒ | Avoid the situation or choose a cold drink that won't be as nice with a biscuit, brush your teeth before dessert. Check menus online beforehand and choose a 'healthier' option in advance so you are not tempted by the menu. Leave one third on your plate. |
| Going food shopping when hungry. | ⇒ | Always shop after you have eaten. Plan a week of meals, write a list and stick to it. Shop online. Take only enough cash. |
| Feeling embarrassed about joining an exercise class. | ⇒ | Go with a friend. Get a DVD to use at home at first. Joining a walking group. |
| Special occasions, such as Christmas, weddings, birthdays, etc. | ⇒ | Plan in advance and allow yourself to eat a little of everything and enjoy it. |
| Feeling like it's never going to work. | ⇒ | Phone a supportive friend and talk through your feelings. |

## TRAFFIC LIGHT SYSTEM

This is a simplified tool based on the transtheoretical model. It is useful if you are short of time as it quickly identifies an individual's attitude towards change. This tool starts with the simple question 'are you ready/do you want to make changes?'

## RESISTANT

It can be tempting to spend time with someone who does not want to change, however, if there is genuine reluctance to making any changes in behaviour, any attempts to overcome this may be met with resistance or denial and can push the individual further from considering change or set them up to fail. If the answer is no, then it is probably best to arrange to meet at a later date and move on to a client who is ambivalent or ready to change and who has a greater chance of success. It is not suggested that you abandon the resistor, merely that you postpone interventions to allow them to consider what you have discussed or become more receptive to change.

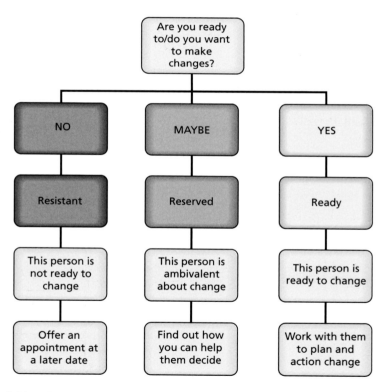

**Figure 7.6** Traffic light system

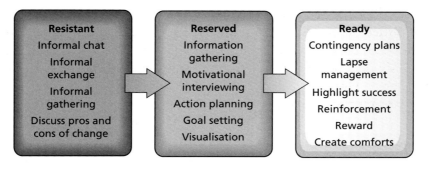

**Figure 7.7** Traffic light flow chart

## RESERVED

Someone who has reservations about change needs time to weigh up the benefits and drawbacks of altering their lifestyle and calculate their confidence in their ability to succeed. Allow them to gather information from you, use techniques such as motivational interviewing or solution focusing to discuss and work through ambivalence to identify and set goals.

## READY

This may appear to be straightforward, as the individual has identified that they are keen to start, however, it can be a difficult step between being ready to make changes and actually making them. Focus on setting goals, contingency plans, lapse management and rewards and keep reminding the client of their reasons for making these changes.

## WRECK

This acronym provides another tool to help with change. It is best used when the client has expressed willingness to change but may have concerns about the process.

- W: Work with the client to weigh up the benefits of changing, get as many positive thoughts as you can.
- R: Assess the risk of making changes, or of starting the same, for example, do they need to consider medication when becoming more active.
- E: Are there existing conditions or injuries that may be exacerbated by activity?
- C: What are the client's concerns, how can these be overcome?

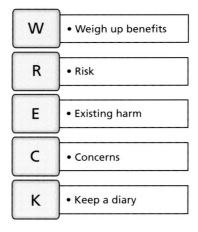

**Figure 7.8** WRECK

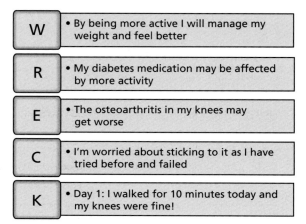

| W | • By being more active I will manage my weight and feel better |
| R | • My diabetes medication may be affected by more activity |
| E | • The osteoarthritis in my knees may get worse |
| C | • I'm worried about sticking to it as I have tried before and failed |
| K | • Day 1: I walked for 10 minutes today and my knees were fine! |

**Figure 7.9** Example completed WRECK

- K: Keeping a diary of what changes are being made, how the client feels or what activities they do can help as it is a permanent record of achievement.

## FIVE As

Used in patient-centred counselling, the Five As is another tool that can be helpful in assisting change. The five steps assist the client in identifying, planning and moving towards change. Use it at the start of the consultation process, ideally when the individual has indicated that they are thinking about change or ready to make changes. Work through the five stages with the individual giving them time to consider their answers.

Assess   Advise   Agree   Assist   Arrange

**Figure 7.10** Five As flowchart

### Assess
In this phase the following can be identified:

- Current health status
- Current beliefs
- Current behaviour patterns
- Knowledge – of risks, benefits, etc.
- Attitude towards making changes

### Advise
Once the client has been assessed, advice can be given on:

- The specific benefits of changing
- Any risks

### Agree
Now it is time to agree the following:

- Confidence to change
- Necessary ability, skills and knowledge
- Goals

### Assist
Once goals and confidence have been identified we can help the client to:

- Identify any barriers to changing
- Design strategies to overcome barriers
- Plan for lapses
- Identify support systems, friends, family, trainers, etc.

### Arrange
Now a follow-up plan can be arranged.

There are some important considerations to make when using the Five As. Goals should be structured and formed in behavioural terms, for example, 'I will walk three times a week', rather than 'I will get rid of my diabetes'. Identify and acknowledge barriers and devise strategies to overcome these; barriers and obstacles can and will occur and ignoring the possibility is setting a client up for failure. The follow-up plan is important, while any intervention needs to be in the control of the client. It is essential they know that there is support there if and when they need it.

## ATTITUDE TO CHANGE

This is a simple questionnaire that can be used to ascertain how ready a person is to change (see Table 7.4). It can be adapted to suit any type of change; however, it is best kept simple to make it easy for the client to use. This links with the transtheoretical model and can identify readiness to change. It should be used at a first meeting or consultation.

Ask the individual to tick which statement best describes their attitude to making changes. Then discuss their answers with them to find out why they feel they are at that stage of change. Use the information gathered to identify any strategies for moving forward.

## PREPARING TO TELL THE STORY – PROBLEMS AND UNUSED OPPORTUNITIES

This is a tool of self-exploration (from Egan 2002:13) and can identify areas where there may be problems or unused resources. This is a useful tool to use at the start of the change process. Use it by getting the client to answer the following statements quickly:

### Problems:

- One of my biggest problems is ...
- I am concerned about ...
- Something I fail to do that gets me into trouble is ...
- The most frequent negative feelings in my life are ...
- These negative feelings arise when ...
- Life would be better if ...
- The person I have most trouble with is ...
- I don't cope very well with ...
- I get anxious when ...
- A value I fail to put into practice is ...
- I am afraid to ...
- I wish I ...

| Table 7.4 | Attitude to change questionnaire |
|---|---|
| **Which of the following statements best describes where you are at the moment?** | |
| 1 | I am not making any changes to my behaviour at the moment and do not intend to start in the next few months |
| 2 | I am not making any changes to my behaviour at the moment but I am thinking about starting in the next few months |
| 3 | I am not making any changes to my behaviour at the moment but I am planning to start in the next month |
| 4 | I have made some small changes in the last month |
| 5 | I have made several changes and maintained them for between one and 5 months |
| 6 | I have made several changes and maintained them for at least six months |

- I wish I didn't ...
- A problem that keeps coming back is ...
- If I could change just one thing in myself, it would be ...

## Opportunities and resources

- Something I like about me is ...
- One thing I do very well is ...
- An example of my caring about others is ...
- People can count on me to ...
- Something I am handling better this year is ...
- A recent temptation I managed to resist was ...
- I am at my best when ...
- I think I have the guts to ...
- If I had one good thing to say about myself, I'd say that ...
- One way I successfully control my emotions is ...
- I communicate most effectively with others when ...

Select key areas the client wishes to discuss and explore with them, while listening actively. This may be difficult to do at first, so choosing one or two key questions may be more comfortable for the practitioner, and the client.

# WHEEL OF BALANCE

This tool can help to identify priorities for life balance and/or identify areas to change to improve balance. It is very broad, so may not be helpful when working with clients who just want to become more active. First, get the client to pick seven (or fewer/more) things that are priorities for their life, these may include areas where they:

- currently direct their energy;
- would like to direct their energy;
- may want to see improvements or change.

Some examples for possible categories are provided in the box below, however, your client may identify their own categories.

NB: It is important for the person to select categories that are important to them.

> Self, spiritual, family, friends, partner, mental health, emotions, social life, exercise, nutrition, medical health, work, study or learning, community, retirement, recreation time, leisure time, hobbies.

1 Next, draw a wheel or pie chart (see Figure 7.11a) and list the names of each category in each pie section.
2 Write a scale of 0 to 10 for each section of the wheel/pie, with 0 at the inside of the circle and 10 on the outside of the circle.
3 Get the client to grade their current satisfaction in each area using the scale to indicate level of current satisfaction (0 in the centre = unsatisfied, to 10 on the outer edge = highly satisfied).
4 Join the dots (see Figure 7.11b). This may highlight areas where life is out of balance.
5 Get the client to grade ideal levels of satisfaction for each area using the same 0–10 scale to represent the level of change they would like to see in each area and that would represent a greater balance for them (see Figure 7.11c).

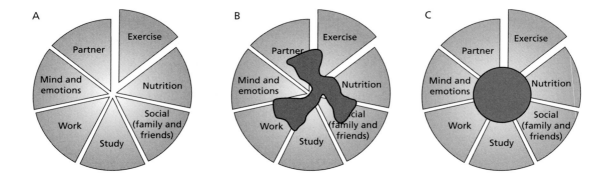

**Figure 7.11a, 7.11b and 7.11c** Wheel of Balance (blank, imbalanced and ideal)

6 Get the client to speak to someone who will listen to discuss their results. There may be lots of areas where they may want to make changes, there may be few. The key is to get the client to identify their own priorities.

7 Get the client to pick one area that is most important to them and where they may like to start making immediate changes, e.g. exercise and activity.

8 Set a goal for the achievement of this change (see previous discussion of goal-setting).

# INNER CRITIC

This tool (from Sunderland and Engleheart 1993) raises awareness of an individual's own negative or self-critical thoughts. It is useful to use at the start of the change process. The client should:

1 Write down some of the negative things they may say about themselves.

2 Discuss their responses with someone they trust and who will listen helpfully.

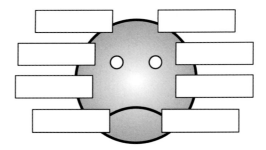

**Figure 7.12** Inner Critic

3 Then, when they notice these thoughts occurring in future, use the thought-stopping technique (see below).

## THOUGHT-STOPPING

Thought-stopping is a simple technique that can be used to stop unwanted or sabotaging thoughts that are in awareness. This technique can be useful in lapse, relapse or collapse situations. It can also be useful to assist motivation and reduce negative thinking spiralling which may lower self-esteem and efficacy. Instructions to the client on how to use this technique are as follows:

121

1 Be aware of the unwanted thought. This requires a mindful awareness of own thinking, which can be developed through mindfulness and mediation practice.
2 Say STOP – out loud or silently and keep saying STOP.
3 You can then thank the thought for popping into your head and replace it with a positive affirmation (see below).

## AFFIRMATIONS

Affirmations are cognitive statements that we can use to encourage and motivate ourselves and can be used to help us improve certain areas of life that we may believe are not working for us. Use affirmations at any time during change to replace any negative self-talk that may prevent achievement of goals, or to replace any inner talk that may reduce a client's own self-esteem.

Affirmations can also be written daily (as well as spoken) as a method of reinforcement. It is essential that they are practised and repeated as often as possible to balance out the negative automatic thoughts (NATs) that can fog the mind.

Get the client to state an area that they would like to change, e.g. valuing self, and frame their affirmations, making sure they follow the guidelines below:

• Be personal (I, my).
• Be positive and use the present tense (already achieved).
• Use action words ('I accept', 'I handle', etc.).
• Use emotion words ('I lovingly').
• Be specific (relationships with self or others, work, activity levels, etc.).
• Be realistic.

• Be confidential (keep them to yourself).

Example affirmations:

• I value, respect and take good care of myself.
• I am powerful, positive and energetic.
• I love to exercise.
• I eat healthy foods.
• I handle all situations positively.
• I feel good about myself.
• All my relationships are harmonious.

## PSYCHOLOGICAL READINESS SCALE/ SCALING

The psychological readiness scale explores the person's readiness to make changes. It should be used at the start of the change process.

It is important to note that different learning styles can be engaged by:

• Auditory: Discussing the scale, asking questions.
• Visual: Using a picture of the scale and asking the person to point or draw where they are.
• Kinaesthetic: Letting the person move along an imaginary scale (between two points in the room, with 1 at one end and 10 at the other end).

Using a 1-10 scale (see Figure 7.13), with 0 = not ready to change and 10 = ready to change, ask your client the following question:

How ready do you feel to start taking action and making the change?'

How ready do you feel to start taking action and making the change?

0 = not ready to change                                        10 = ready to change

**Figure 7.13** Psychological readiness scale

Example dialogue could be: 'OK, you have told me that you would like to start being more active and suggested that you could make a start by going for a lunchtime walk for 15 minutes. How ready do you feel (using the 1–10 scale) to start taking action?'

Once the person has indicated where they feel they are, ask additional probing questions to explore their motivation. For example:

- You have indicated that you are a 5 on the scale, where would you like to be?
- You have said you would like to be around 7 or 8, what would help to move you to this score?

These additional questions may help to identify the change and sustain talk that the client uses. Change and sustain talk are explained in Chapter 3 (see Table 3.7) and are important because change talk helps the person make the changes, while sustain talk keeps the person stuck in their current behaviour.

A sample conversation is given below:

Practitioner: On a scale of 1–10, how do you feel about starting to walk more often?

Client: Probably 6?

Practitioner: Why 6?

Client: Well 5 is halfway and I feel more than halfway ready [smiles]. I joined a walking group last week.

Practitioner: So you joined a walking group and that feels good, more than halfway?

C: Yes [smiles again].

Practitioner: Why not lower?

Client: Well I know I can walk for about 30 minutes without stopping, there will be people in the group with my condition and my friend has been along and she is about the same level as me.

Practitioner: So you feel ready and walking is something you want to do?

Client: Yes.

Practitioner: If you were walking regularly, where would you be on the scale?

Client: Probably about 8.

Practitioner: How would 8 feel?

Client: I would feel that I was making time for me then, to do something good for me.

## RECOGNISING OBSTACLES (RISKS FOR LAPSE)

Every change process will raise a number of obstacles or barriers that may prevent achievement. It is useful to be aware of some of those barriers in advance, so that strategies to overcome the barriers of obstacles can be put into place. This strategy is useful at any stage of change. To use it, get the client to:

1 Draw a pathway and indicate the start, middle and end points of the journey (see Figure 7.14):
   - Start – where are you now?
   - Middle – what measure would indicate a positive movement?
   - End – what would be the ideal outcome?
   - The pathway can be straight, squiggly, circular. Get the client to pick a shape that feels right for their journey.
2 Write down all the blocks and obstacles they may face, anything that may stop them from making a change; things that will get in their way; obstacles they may need to overcome.
3 Write down all the ways they can avoid or manage the barriers. This may include, going over, going around, going under or busting right through the middle.
4 Write down the resources (inner and outer) that they may need to help them move through these barriers
5 Be creative and draw, paint or create a collage of their change process. They can add words, pictures, colour – anything that they find inspirational and meaningful.
6 Discuss the client's pathway and collage with them.

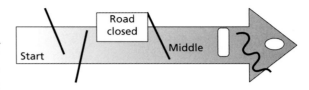

**Figure 7.14** Overcoming obstacles

### Example: Barriers to starting walking
- Gate 1 – tired.
- Gate 2 – have to work late.
- Road closed – children ill.
- Gate 3 – can't be bothered.
- Obstacle – raining.
- Obstacle – not feeling well.
- Obstacle – telling self will start tomorrow.

By drawing all potential obstacles and barriers, the person can be helped to explore ways to overcome these.

### Strategies
- Schedule walking into my day – e.g. book an appointment.
- Tell self I will feel better after.
- Walk at lunchtime.
- Do another activity at home.
- Go with a friend.
- Let yourself have a day off.

## EXPLORING SUPPORT SYSTEMS/ENERGY TANKS

This is a strategy to help recognise areas of a client's life that need to be replenished through inner and external support systems to maintain their energy levels. It can be used at any time during the process of change.

It works by getting the client to imagine that from the time they wake up, until the time they go to sleep, they have a number of pots of 'energy' that come from different sources. These tanks need to be refilled regularly, much like a car needs petrol/fuel to keep running. Different people will have different energy needs.

For example, if I feel hungry, I need to restock my *nutritional* energy tank, so I must eat something. If I feel sad, I may need to speak with someone or go and have a hot bath by candlelight, or do something that feels soothing to nurture my *emotional* energy tank. Instructions to the client would be as follows:

1   Write a list of all the ways that you:
    • Give to and fill your energy tanks. List positive strategies for doing this.
    • Take from and deplete your energy tanks. List negative behaviours.

2   Write a list of all the ways that other people:
    • Give to and nurture your energy tanks. List your energy radiators.
    • Take from and deplete your energy tanks. List your energy drainers.
3   Discuss your findings with someone you trust and who listens fully.
4   Reflect on any changes you may like to make.
5   Set a goal to make a change in this area (see earlier discussion of goal-setting).

## CREATURE COMFORTS/ REWARDS

Creature comforts are the things we do to make ourselves feel good or better. Creature comforts may form a reward for goal achievement and most of the things we do to make ourselves feel good will be positive.

However, some of the things we do to make ourselves feel good may potentially have a negative impact on our health. It is necessary to be aware of the risks attached to certain behaviours so that we

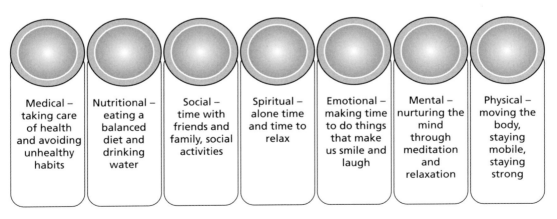

**Figure 7.15** Energy tanks

| Table 7.5 | Creature comforts | | |
|---|---|---|---|
| **Creature comforts** | **Any risks attached** | **Level of harm** | **Likelihood of risk** |
| | **Self or others** | **Low------------------Medium--------------------High** | |
| Hot bubble bath with candlelight *Helps me to relax and unwind* | Only if the bath is too hot or I fall asleep | Low | Low |
| Reading a book *Takes my mind off other things* | None | Low | Low |
| Snuggle on the sofa and watch a movie | Health risks attached to excess sedentary behaviour | Low – I only do this occasionally | Low |
| Going for a walk *Takes my mind off other things* | Traffic Crossing roads | High if I get hit! | Low |
| Smoking a cigarette *To cope with stress* | Health risks attached to cigarette smoking | High – this is a habit | High |
| Having a glass of wine *Helps me to relax and unwind* | Heath risks attached to excess alcohol intake | Low if I stay within recommended guidelines | Low normally, high when out with friends |

can then choose whether we sustain these behaviours, or contemplate changing these behaviours in some way. A basic risk assessment tool can be used to assess the risk attached to certain behaviours. Instructions to the client should be as follows:

1   Write a list of all the things you do or would like to do and that make you feel good about yourself.
2   Make a note of how these activities may contribute to your energy levels (e.g. how they make you feel and how they help you – the positives).
3   Make a note of the potential risks attached to

these behaviours and the level and likelihood of risk (the negatives).
4   Reflect on what you have written and write down how you feel and what you think (this may reflect inner self-talk).

# BEHAVIOUR CHANGE ACTION PLAN

This is a written action plan that looks at specific aspects of the change process and identifies supporters and obstacles. Use this when setting goals. Get the individual to complete the plan, working with them to identify and prepare for any barriers or obstacles.

## Table 7.6  Action plan

| | |
|---|---|
| Name: | Date: |

**My outcome goal is:**

**My process goals are:**

| Goal: | Time: |
|---|---|
| | |
| | |
| | |

**My action plan is:**

| | |
|---|---|
| Where am I going to do this? | |
| When am I going to do it? | |
| Who am I going to do it with? | |
| How will I keep track of my progress? | |

**Barriers to success**

| | |
|---|---|
| Environment: is there anything in my environment that may be an obstacle? | What can I do to change this? |
| People: are there people I spend time with who might make it difficult for me? | What can I do to change this? |
| Thoughts and feelings: is there anything I am thinking or feeling that may make it difficult for me? | What can I do to change this? |

**Aids to success**

| | |
|---|---|
| Environment: is there anything in my environment that may be helpful? | What can I do to make the most of this? |
| People: are there any people around me who may be helpful? | How can I ask them to help me? |
| Thoughts and feelings: is there anything I am thinking or feeling that may be helpful? | How can I encourage these thoughts and feelings? |

## CALCULATING CONFIDENCE

Confidence and self-efficacy are important in both successful change and in adhering to that change. As previously discussed, the right goal can help to boost confidence and will also create motivation. That is why it is so important to ensure that the goal is actually something the person really wants. Confidence calculating can be used when setting goals at the start of the process of change.

Get the individual to write down their goal. Now ask the questions on each stage. If the answer to the first question is in the 1–3 zone, the goal is probably not the right one at this time, so suggest the individual considers another goal or reworks the goal to make it more desirable.

If confidence is in the 4–7 zone for the second question, ask the client why they are at that level and not lower down the scale. The intention is to build on existing confidence and help the individual move into the 8–9 zone.

If confidence is in the 8–9 zone, then confidence is high and strategies to maintain this can be developed.

The confidence calculation technique can also be used to identify solutions and skills that the person has. Asking the client 'why have you given a score of 5 and not one of, say, 3?' can give you an indication of the abilities the person believes they have and this can then be used in planning the best next step to get to a higher level on the scale.

In motivational interviewing, this calculator is used to assess importance and confidence, as people who are high on importance but low on confidence will need encouragement to see that change is possible and support to generate ideas on how to do it. Those high on confidence but low on importance need to look at why they have selected that particular goal and may need to consider if it is important enough to work towards.

## I-CAN

In simple terms this is based on self-efficacy and confidence – the underlying principle is the belief that 'I CAN do this'. Adapted from various motivational theories and models, including *The Art of Making a Difference* (Gilbert 2001) this is a seven-step process to setting, adopting and achieving goals. The initial focus is on motivation and goal-setting, then the focus shifts to priorities and self-belief and finally the focus is on personal responsibility and support from others. It can be used at any time and with any goal, however large or small. Ask the individual to complete the following grid.

| My goal is |
|---|

| Confidence calculator 1–importance |
|---|

| On a scale of 1 to 10, how much do you want this goal? |
|---|

| 1 | 2 | 3 | 4 | 5 | 6 | 7 | 8 | 9 | 10 |
|---|---|---|---|---|---|---|---|---|---|

| Not a lot | More than anything |
|---|---|

| Confidence calculator 2–self-belief |
|---|

| Do you believe you can achieve this goal |
|---|

| 1 | 2 | 3 | 4 | 5 | 6 | 7 | 8 | 9 | 10 |
|---|---|---|---|---|---|---|---|---|---|

| No | Yes |
|---|---|

| Confidence calculator 3–sticking to it |
|---|

| Are you confident that when you achieve this goal you will maintain it? |
|---|

| 1 | 2 | 3 | 4 | 5 | 6 | 7 | 8 | 9 | 10 |
|---|---|---|---|---|---|---|---|---|---|

| No | Yes |
|---|---|

**Figure 7.16** Confidence calculator

| Table 7.7a | I-CAN grid | |
|---|---|---|
| I | Identify | Identify your goal<br>Identify how important the goal is<br>Define it using SMART or other methods |
| C | Create confidence | Check confidence in ability to achieve the goal<br>Build self-efficacy in ability to achieve the goal<br>Focus on past successes |
| A | Action | Make a list of at least 20 things you can do to help achieve the goal<br>Enlist support of others who can help you<br>Plan for lapses<br>Start making changes<br>Take personal responsibility for your actions |
| N | Notes | Make a note of your goal<br>Write down a reward for achieving the goal<br>Keep notes of achievements and feelings<br>Tell everyone when you get there! |

| Table 7.7b | Example I-CAN answers | |
|---|---|---|
| I | Identify | To complete the 5k Race for Life in four months<br>I want to raise money for charity in memory of a relative |
| C | Create confidence | My confidence is 9 out of 10<br>I know I can do this as I can already run 2k |
| A | Action | Start training<br>Follow a training programme<br>Get a buddy<br>Sign up for the race<br>Find a running track or gym when I'm away in a month |
| N | Notes | My goal is on my screensaver<br>I will treat myself to a spa day after the race<br>I know I can do this! |

# TRIGGER IDENTIFICATION AND PLANNING (TRIP)

Trips or lapses are a normal part of change. No one is perfect all the time and the occasional lapse, as discussed previously, is part of life. How these lapses are managed to prevent relapse is an important factor in change. Knowing what triggers exist and developing coping strategies may help avoid relapse. Trigger identification and planning is ideally used during the process of change if and when lapses occur.

Work with the individual to identify any lapses from change and then plan ways to overcome these lapses if the trigger is encountered again.

| Table 7.8a | TRIP questions | | |
|---|---|---|---|
| **Trigger** | **Response** | **Impact** | **Plan** |
| Before the behaviour:<br>What were you doing?<br>What were you thinking?<br>What were you feeling?<br>Who were you with?<br>Where were you? | What did you do? | What happened after this?<br>How did you feel? | What will you do next time? |

| Table 7.8b | Example TRIP responses | | |
|---|---|---|---|
| **Trigger** | **Response** | **Impact** | **Plan** |
| Friend's birthday where there was a buffet and open bar | Ate too much and drank too much | Felt sick, had a hangover<br>Felt I had let myself down and was ashamed<br>Thought I had blown my new behaviours | Next time I will stick to gin and tonic (smaller measures than wine), with lots of tonic, and stand well away from the buffet table to avoid overeating |

# IF ... THEN

This is a planning tool that can help people adhere to new behaviours and avoid or plan for triggers for lapses. It is a useful tool to use throughout the change process. Fill in the sentence 'If ... then ...' to identify any obstacles, triggers or weaknesses the individual has and then develop strategies to avoid or overcome these.

| Table 7.9 | Example of 'If ... then' planning |
|---|---|
| If I buy a sandwich for lunch<br>Then I will buy a piece of fruit instead of a bag of crisps |
| If I am going out with friends<br>Then I will choose a healthy option from the menu |
| If I am away and miss my regular swim<br>Then I will go for a walk instead |

## THE MIRACLE QUESTION OR LOOK TO FUTURE

This can be used for people to examine the implication of change, or to help develop an action plan. The question can be asked in a number of ways:

- Let's imagine that you have become more active, how would you feel?
- If you woke up tomorrow and everything had changed, how would it feel/look?
- If you could wave a magic wand, what would change?
- I wonder how this change will feel to you?

## SUMMARY

There are many more tools that can be used to help a client move forward through change. When working with clients, it is the role of the practitioner to identify which will be the most motivational tools and help the client to use these in their change process.

The following diagram illustrates the process of putting it into practice:

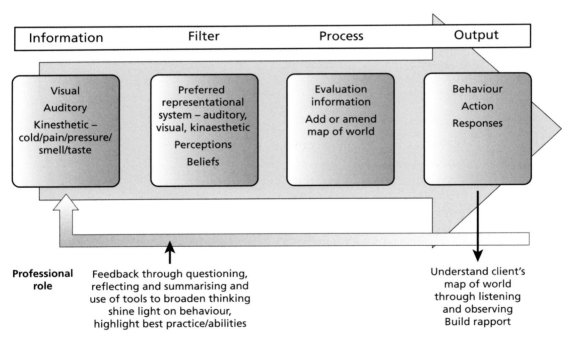

| Information | Filter | Process | Output |

| Visual<br>Auditory<br>Kinesthetic – cold/pain/pressure/smell/taste | Preferred representational system – auditory, visual, kinaesthetic<br>Perceptions<br>Beliefs | Evaluation information<br>Add or amend map of world | Behaviour<br>Action<br>Responses |

**Professional role**

Feedback through questioning, reflecting and summarising and use of tools to broaden thinking shine light on behaviour, highlight best practice/abilities

Understand client's map of world through listening and observing Build rapport

**Figure 7.17** The process

## KEY POINTS

- As with models and theories, no one tool provides a best fit for any client.
- Clients may find different tools or strategies motivational at different stages of change.
- Approaches may need to be changed or adapted if they no longer appeal to the client.
- Practitioners can devise any tool or approach that they feel will benefit the client.

Ultimately, the client is responsible for change, not the practitioner or the approach or strategy.

# SECTION THREE

## THE APPLICATION

### INTRODUCTION

Having considered the background, psychology and tools associated with the lifestyle behaviour change process, this section looks at putting it into practice in a range of settings. Also considered are the implications for change for specific client groups and settings.

The aims of this section are to:

- Consider a client-centred approach to lifestyle change.

- Adapt models and interventions to suit a range of settings and clients.
- Utilise tools and strategies to assist clients in changing behaviour.
- Consider implications for a range of settings, including:
  - Health and specialist settings; exercise referral, clinics, etc.
  - Mainstream settings; the gym, personal training, etc.
  - Amateur sport

# PUTTING IT INTO PRACTICE

## 8

It would be so nice to be able provide a 'perfect' approach to behaviour change but the reality is that there is no 'one size fits all' model or approach that exists. Each client will have different thoughts, needs and goals and will require different approaches to support them in making sustainable changes. Therefore, the best approach is probably a client-centred one – in other words, start with the client and build an approach round them.

There are, however, some simple guidelines that can be adapted easily in a range of settings and with different clients and this chapter considers these and builds on the information provided in previous chapters.

## A SIMPLE PATHWAY

This pathway is a simple summary of the information in the previous sections. It is not intended as a fixed tool, rather as a set of suggestions to enhance client-centred working. Each client will differ in both readiness and willingness to change and as the practitioner becomes more experienced, it will be easier to identify the appropriate skills and tools that will suit the situation and person. However, this pathway provides a useful starting point.

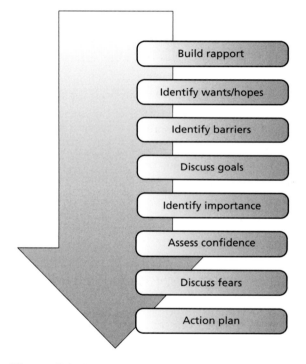

**Figure 8.1** A simple pathway

## BUILD RAPPORT

Rapport-building is perhaps the most important factor in assisting clients to make lasting lifestyle changes. The communication skills outlined in

Chapter 6 are important in building rapport, particularly with clients who are initially resistant to the idea of change.

Consider how the initial meeting is set up. A phone call will enable the practitioner to introduce themselves and explain what the initial meeting is all about and ask if the client has anything they want to discuss or what they expect to happen at the meeting. This initial contact serves to set the agenda and will give the client useful information and help them to prepare for the meeting. Many clients believe that their first meeting will involve using equipment or taking part in a class, which creates nervousness, so explaining what is going to happen will reassure them.

Meeting the client at reception on their first visit is worthwhile as walking through busy areas full of people who know what they are doing can be daunting and it is often easy to get lost in larger facilities.

Other considerations include the setting; try and carry out initial assessments and screening in a private, quiet area. Sitting in the middle of a noisy gym environment is not conducive to conversation, let alone building rapport. Also consider the images or posters on the walls, how you are dressed and, if you are making notes, that they have access to these so they are comfortable with what is being written. Avoid interruptions as they may interfere with the process of rapport building.

## SET AGENDA

It is important for the practitioner to start the process of setting the agenda but let the client take over and identify what they want to discuss. Being open and enquiring will help the client to explore what they want and identify any issues with progress. Open questions, active listening and positive body language are crucial to encourage this. Start with an open question about what the client wants to talk about before completing any forms or assessments as this will help the client relax and help the practitioner start to understand the client.

## IDENTIFY WANTS AND HOPES

It is useful to start by finding out what the client wants, hopes for or expects from making changes to their lifestyle. This enables the practitioner to identify the client's true wants and also to spot any unrealistic expectations such as giving up alcohol, quitting smoking, becoming active and making drastic changes to their diet – by tomorrow! Use open questions and ask what they hope to gain from the meeting, even if they don't know, this shows that they are at the centre of the process.

Often clients present wants or needs that they feel they 'should' or 'ought' to work towards or change as opposed to what they really want or feel able to do.

## IDENTIFY IMPORTANCE

Having identified wants and hopes it is important to assess how important the outcome is to the client. As discussed in the previous paragraph, these may not be intrinsically important to the client so it is crucial to identify what the client really wants so that these can be developed into goals that will motivate and excite them. They may be reluctant to admit their true goals for fear of seeming superficial, but it is important to identify these and show the client that whether they start to be more active for medical reasons or for vanity, health benefits will occur and the outcome that is most important to them, whether it is being healthier or looking better, will create and sustain the motivation to keep going.

Ask how important the outcome is to the client, why it is important and how they feel about making the necessary changes. This will help identify their readiness to change and may give you ideas for strategies to use to support them.

## ASSESS CONFIDENCE

However important the outcome, a lack of confidence in the ability to succeed may override the perceived benefits to be gained. The confidence calculator is a useful tool to use when discussing importance and confidence and the lower score is the most important to focus on initially. If the level of importance and confidence are similar, start with importance and if both are low it may be worth exploring why they have identified this want as it may be extrinsic (or a 'should') rather than something they really want.

Ask the client to recall past successes to reinforce confidence, however small. Older adults may have successfully adopted the habit of putting on a seatbelt when they get in a car or they may have stopped smoking or started to take their own bags to the supermarket each time. Focusing on these past successes helps to build confidence in present ability.

## IDENTIFY BARRIERS

Rollnick et al (1999) refer to reducing resistance. Barriers and fears are forms of resistance that are often used as excuses for not trying, perhaps because of a fear of failure or, conversely, a fear of success. The phrase 'yes, but …' will be commonly heard and is an indication that resistance is occurring. Why does resistance occur? Often resistance is the result of the client feeling a lack of control or choice, not wanting to make the change, or not valuing the outcome; or of the practitioner

misjudging how important the outcome is and how confident or ready the client feels about making the change and 'forcing' the client towards change.

The steps above work towards reducing resistance by placing the client at the centre of the process and giving them control. This involves identifying barriers to change, both real and perceived, and working with the client to minimise or overcome these.

Barriers may be intrinsic or extrinsic to the client. Extrinsic barriers, such as a lack of time, a large young family or working long hours, will need to be worked around rather than being changed – as any mother knows it is not possible to change some elements of family life – while intrinsic feelings of low self-efficacy or fear of failure may be 'easier' to change, albeit slowly. It is important to identify barriers early so that they can be worked with or overcome; ignoring them will make 'failure' more likely.

## DISCUSS FEARS

Fear can hold even the most determined person back and it is not just fear of failure, but fear of success. Fear of success may need further exploration with more qualified professionals but is a factor in motivation.

We have all heard people say that if they could just lose that extra weight they are carrying, everything would be fantastic, their life would change for the better; it is their weight that is holding them back. So why don't they lose it? Surely the anticipated or expected outcome is worth the effort? This is where fear of success kicks in, what if, having lost the weight, life was the same? The person would then have to accept the fact that it is factors intrinsic to them that are responsible, not the weight, and that may be too hard to face. This is where a practitioner's role ends and that of a counsellor begins, so it is important to maintain boundaries and avoid crossing into other areas of support for which you are not qualified.

## SET GOALS

The steps so far help to identify wants, needs, importance, confidence, fears and barriers. Once this is accomplished, effective goal-setting can take place. As throughout the process, the client is at the centre of this, so goals should be in their words and reflect their valued outcome. Goal-setting has been discussed fully in Section 2 and practitioners only need to guide and help shape realistic goals at this stage. Consider setting process goals focused on positive behaviour changes, such as to swap one unhealthy snack for a healthy one each day, rather than outcome goals, such as losing two pounds a week, to foster a sense of success, particularly with weight as this can fluctuate daily!

## ACTION PLAN

Once goals are set, it is time to plan. A good action plan takes goals, confidence and potential lapses into account and starts with small steps towards the eventual outcome, increasing gradually with each successful achievement.

## SUMMARY

This is a simple pathway designed to support the practitioner in helping the client. As such, it is intended to be a flexible method that the practitioner can adapt to suit their own style or their client's needs. As always, practice is key. Start slowly and build gradually while you become familiar with the process and can learn how to adapt it to suit a range of situations and clients.

## KEY POINTS

- Building rapport is key to successful communication.
- Communication is essential to build rapport!
- Allow time for the client to identify their wants as well as their barriers.
- Assess importance in goals and confidence in ability to achieve them.
- Discuss and plan to overcome fears.
- Devise an action plan that works towards goals, accounts for barriers and suits the client's readiness and confidence to change.

# HEALTH AND SPECIALIST SETTINGS

# 9

Exercise is increasingly promoted for prevention of chronic disease, reduction of disease risk and as treatment or management in established conditions. It is essential for any instructor working in this field to be appropriately qualified not only in exercise referral but also in any specialist conditions with which they may work. The new Level 4 qualifications are designed to enhance clients' health and recovery from or management of disease and build on the knowledge and skills gained at Level 3.

The aims of this chapter are to:

- Identify personnel and settings involved in health behaviour change.
- Outline the role of exercise referral schemes.
- Outline strategies for dealing with clients who are resistant, reluctant or ready for change.
- Give examples of constructive and obstructive conversations that may occur.

## THE MULTIDISCIPLINARY TEAM

Working with clients with health conditions or increased risk factors in a referral or clinical setting usually means working with a multidisciplinary team (MDT). The role of the MDT is for professionals from two or more clinical fields to work together to decide on appropriate treatment for individual patients. It must be remembered that health professionals are highly qualified and skilled individuals and have specific knowledge in the condition and their client's medical history. As a fitness professional or sports coach, it is imperative that you do not cross the boundary into clinical advice as this lies outside your role and may contradict medical advice or recommendation.

Some key health professionals you may work with as part of a MDT include:

### General practitioner (GP)
The GP is usually the first person involved in diagnosis and referral in primary care and their role is identification of a condition and discussion of treatment options, including referral for exercise. The GP, as part of their role in general practice, provides a wide range of care services in the local community and helps patients to understand and take responsibility for their own health.

## Practice nurse

The practice nurse is part of the primary health care team, usually in a GP surgery or clinic. They help with most aspects of patient treatment and care and may perform routine tasks including vaccinations, health screening and running smoking cessation programmes. They may refer low-risk patients to referral schemes for activity and are a good contact if there are any queries about a referred client.

## Physiotherapist

The role of the physiotherapist is to work with people who have problems with movement as a result of illness, injury, etc. They work in a variety of settings including community- and clinical-based environments, leisure and sport services and private clinics. Physiotherapists work with a range of patients to improve movement potential and help with quality of life and functional ability. They are increasingly involved in the community and may refer into exercise referral schemes. If this is the case, it is recommended that instructors ask for information about any exercises that have already been done to provide continuity of treatment.

## Occupational therapist

An occupational therapist (OT) works in a variety of clinical and outpatient settings and their key role is to help individuals to learn, or relearn, the skills needed for daily life in self-care, domestic, social and work areas through activities that promote skills and confidence. They work with a range of conditions including: neurological conditions such as Parkinson's disease and motor neurone disease; mental health conditions; post-stroke and after trauma.

## Midwife

Midwives work with pregnant women and their partners and families to help maintain and promote physical and mental health during pregnancy. They work with clients through pregnancy, from confirmation to birth and beyond. In cases where a pregnant woman has a chronic disease or disability, mental health condition, or is obese, they are a vital link and instructors should seek advice on proposed activity programmes before they start to work with pregnant clients.

## Cardiac rehabilitation team

Cardiac rehabilitation has four stages. Stage 1 occurs in an inpatient setting soon after a cardiac event such as myocardial infarction or surgery. It involves assessment of physical and mental conditions and any risk factors together with education and reassurance of misconceptions and allaying any fears. Initial mobilisation also occurs in Stage 1.

Stage 2 occurs in the early stages following discharge, and involves support and the identification of any anxiety or depression following the event.

A structured exercise programme, usually comprising low to moderate intensity aerobic activity in a clinical or supervised setting forms the basis of Stage 3. Smoking cessation and dietary advice are also important in this phase.

Stage 4 consolidates the changes in lifestyle that have been promoted and started in Stages 1 to 3. Stage 4 instructors, sometimes referred to by the acronym BACPR (British Association for Cardiovascular Prevention and Rehabilitation), work with clients to deliver physical activity in community settings, alongside other cardiac rehabilitation clients, which provides motivation and support. Stage 4 instructors usually hold a qualification in exercise referral and are experienced in a wide range of fitness disciplines.

### Dietician

A dietician specialises in nutrition and may work in the NHS or in private or public environments such as schools or the food industry. As well as providing information and education to individuals, community groups and the public, they work with clients who have specific dietary needs, including food allergies, obesity, eating disorders, diabetes, gastrointestinal problems and conditions, oncology and kidney disease. They are highly trained, having a degree in nutrition and dietetics as a minimum qualification.

### Diabetes nurse

Diabetes nurses are specialists in education for people who have new or established diabetes or whose condition has changed. They work to help people to manage their diabetes and treatment. They may advise on diet, exercise and other lifestyle-related behaviours.

### Cancer nurse

Cancer nurses are employed by the NHS but posts may be funded initially by charities such as Macmillan. They work exclusively with cancer patients to help manage the condition and treatment or to provide practical and emotional support to the individual and their family.

### Community mental health team

The community mental health team (CMHT) comprises a range of health care professionals working together to deliver mental health services in the community. Key professionals within the team are the psychiatrist, counsellor/psychologist, community psychiatric nurse and care coordinator.

## EXERCISE REFERRAL SCHEMES

Exercise referral is an increasing area in health and fitness instruction and raises some issues regarding readiness to change. It is vital for any practitioner in this field to have an appropriate Level 3 or Level 4 qualification and to maintain that status through relevant continuing professional development (CPD). It is common for clients to be in pre-contemplation. They may well have been referred for exercise by their doctor or other health care professional despite having no interest in activity and may be experiencing a double concern – that of having a health problem alongside the fear of being active!

Clients may be referred into schemes by their doctor/GP, a practice nurse, physiotherapist, osteopath, occupational therapist, consultant or other medical professional. Clients considered suitable for referral may have mild to moderate, well-controlled conditions such as:

- Coronary heart disease
- Hypertension
- Atherosclerosis
- Diabetes, Type 1 and 2
- Osteoarthritis
- Rheumatoid arthritis
- Simple lower back pain
- Osteoporosis
- Obesity
- Depression, stress or anxiety
- Asthma

- Chronic obstructive pulmonary disease
- Multiple sclerosis
- Parkinson's disease

Clients may also be referred if they have risk factors for conditions such as coronary heart disease and/or are sedentary. Clients with cardiac conditions or more severe or less well-controlled conditions will be referred to instructors who hold a higher level qualification (Level 4) in a specific condition range. Currently Level 4 qualifications exist in:

- Cardiac rehabilitation
- Falls prevention
- Diabetes and obesity
- Mental health
- Back pain
- Cancer
- Chronic respiratory disease
- Stroke
- Long-term neurological conditions
- Accelerated military rehabilitation (only available in the military)

When an individual turns up to the gym or class or books a session with a personal trainer, they are usually ready to at least consider change, however, referred clients may be there because their GP or another health professional has told them to attend. Often in the medical setting, people are patients who are 'done to', while in exercise referral settings we see them as clients who are going to 'do it themselves'. This may mean they are actually a pre-contemplator who does not intend or want to make changes at the moment, or their expectation may be that the practitioner is going to sort it all out for them. They may have visited their doctor in the expectation of a quick diagnosis and helpful prescription only to be told they need to exercise – possibly for the first time in years! The double blow of being told they are at risk of or already have a condition (which is worrying enough) together with the thought of attending the gym (in Lycra) can be overwhelming and prevent communication around health behaviour change rather than aid it.

## THE RESISTANT CLIENT

Someone who is resistant is not interested in changing their activity habits at this time. They may be unaware of the risks of being inactive or have decided to ignore the risks. It can be difficult to work with these clients as they are likely to be very resistant to the idea of change and are likely to have convinced themselves that their current lifestyle is fine. Alternatively, they may believe that having a health problem is a sign of weakness and may see any advice as unwelcome interference that makes them more determined to stay as they are. It is likely that they have come to see you because they have been referred for activity by a health professional, so they may also be dealing with mixed emotions around their health.

Your aim at this stage is to help the individual realise that their current lifestyle might be a problem, either now or in the future, and to guide them towards considering making a change. However, if the client is determined to ignore or disregard any health issues it may be best to let them go – they are more likely to consider issues if they are not forced to.

Strategies that may be useful in this stage are:

## Informal chat

An informal chat is just that, a chat. It is not lecturing or telling off or giving unwanted advice, merely a chance to find out what the client feels and knows about his or her health. The key is to keep it informal by avoiding giving advice, scaring the client or making them feel inadequate.

Use positive communication skills such as open questions and active listening to encourage the client to discuss their lifestyle. Avoid giving your opinions or beliefs or trying to force them to see things 'in the right way'. Open questions will encourage fuller answers and help reveal the thoughts the client has about health issues and activity and it is important to allow them to reach their own conclusions in their own time. The aim is to help the client to reveal and discuss intrinsic thoughts that will, in turn, help you to discover why they are reluctant to admit a problem or consider change.

## Information exchange

Discussed in more detail in the section on motivational interviewing in Chapter 3, the informal chat can be used to exchange information. The client may have questions to ask you and you can ask questions to gain information and insight into the client's current state of mind and readiness to change. However, the key is to allow the client to volunteer information at their own pace and ask (and receive answers to) any questions they may have.

Consider the following conversations:

Practitioner: Your current levels of activity are very low, you are not meeting the guidelines for health and really should be doing more.

Client: I do as much as I can, I'm not unfit and anyway, I don't have time.

Practitioner: Do you really think you are fine? You are overweight and you blood pressure is high.

Client: My family are big boned and, anyway, the dietician I saw was much bigger than me and she is the expert.

Practitioner: Take it from me, you are not OK and are heading for lots of health problems and maybe even an early death if you don't start taking better care of yourself.

Client: I don't see how taking up exercising will help. I know lots of people who got injured doing that.

Practitioner: Yes, but …

This starts as a negative conversation and goes downhill rapidly from there. Confronting the client with scare tactics is more likely to send them running (slowly) in the opposite direction. Now consider the following example:

Practitioner: Your current activity levels seem quite low, how do you feel about that?

Client: I do as much as I can. I'm not unfit and, anyway, I don't have time.

Practitioner: Is there anything you would like to do if you did have the time?

Client: I don't really like the gym, all that Lycra …

Practitioner: I can't say I blame you … is there anything else that you might like?

Client: I used to go dancing but the class closed and I never got round to finding another.

Practitioner: Dancing is fun, isn't it? And I bet you felt like you'd done something active as well.

Client: Actually, yes, I always felt really good after the class as well. It would be fun to do that again.

Practitioner: Did you know there are a couple of classes nearby? Would you be interested in finding out more?

From a negative start the practitioner has found something that may appeal and will get the individual thinking about restarting.

## THE RELUCTANT CLIENT

Often an individual may be aware that their lifestyle could be improved or that there are health risks linked to their current activity. They may have been pondering doing something 'soon' or may just not know where to start or they may have attempted to make changes in the past and been unsuccessful. Equally, they may not have given much thought to what they really want to achieve.

The aim in this stage is to identify the barriers and highlight the benefits of changing and move the client towards making a change. Useful strategies in this stage include:

### Information-gathering

The aim of information-gathering is to discover how the client feels about activity and discover why they are not doing much. It can also be used to give information about the benefits of exercise and activity on general well-being. As with all clients, it is important to allow them to make the suggestions and come up with their own plan. Examples of positive and negative conversations are given below:

Practitioner: Tell me about the activity you do at the moment.

Client: I'm not really doing anything, I don't really have the time.

Practitioner: Everyone has time; you just need to manage it better. It's important if you want to improve your health.

Client: Well I don't have time, what am I supposed to give up – work, sleep? Anyway I run around all day after the kids.

Practitioner: You won't help your health if you don't make time, which is more important to you, health or TV?

Client: Well I'm hardly ever ill, so I'm clearly fine.

Practitioner: Yes, but …

Another negative and probably frustrating conversation that is unlikely to change the client's mind about activity, so let us consider changing the focus:

Practitioner: Tell me about the activity you do at the moment.

Client: I'm not really doing anything, I don't really have the time.

Practitioner: OK, tell me about your average day, what do you do?

Client: Well, I get everyone up and make breakfast then take the kids to the bus stop at the end of the road. After that, I drive to work where I sit at my desk all day working on the computer. I usually grab a sandwich at my desk then drive to pick up the kids from after-school club, then go home, cook supper for everyone, do some washing and housework and then watch a bit of telly and fall into bed.

Practitioner: That sounds like a very busy day, I can see how you feel it would be hard to fit something else in.

Client: Absolutely, I think I should do something though, shouldn't I? It's just so hard to find the time.

Practitioner: I wonder if we could just discuss how much time you think you need to exercise for?

Client: It's about an hour every day isn't it? I definitely don't have an hour.

Practitioner: Actually, it's much less than that for health. The aim is 150 minutes in a week which could be half an hour on five days a week or ten minutes a day and a long walk at the weekend or any combination, whatever fits your lifestyle.

Client: Wow, ten minutes doesn't sound too hard, I didn't know I could do it in bits like that. I might even be able to do something in a lunchtime. What sort of things could I do?

From a potentially negative start, the client has started to gain information and is showing an interest in doing something so the conversation can start to move towards goals.

## THE READY CLIENT

It is with great joy that we welcome the client who says they are ready, willing and keen to make changes and it is often assumed that this client, because they are preparing for change or may have even started, is the easy one. Not so. Often the 'readiness' is superficial and coupled with many 'excuses' for not starting 'today'.

Key at this stage is building self-efficacy and creating a valued outcome. This can be done through goal-setting, action planning and visualising the end result.

Practitioner: So you have said you are keen to get going with some exercise, can you tell me what would you like to achieve from this?

Client: Well, I want to get fit.

Practitioner: Fantastic, let's get you started as soon as possible. Here is the gym. We are going to set up your induction and write a programme and you can get going.

Client: Great, I'll reach my goal in no time.

Practitioner: You will. If you have any questions at any time let me know.

(several weeks later at the midpoint)

Practitioner: So how is it going?

Client: Well, I've been trying to come along but it doesn't seem to be working, I don't feel any fitter.

Practitioner: Well, if you have been coming regularly then you must be fitter, even if you don't notice …

Not very motivational, the client has no idea if they are fitter. Any measurement of the aim is subjective and they are not going to feel supported by the practitioner.

Practitioner: So you have said you are keen to get going with some exercise, can you tell me what would you like to achieve from this?

Client: Well, I want to get fit.

Practitioner: OK, that's great. Can you just tell me how will you know when you are fitter?

Client: Um, well I guess I'll feel fitter!

Practitioner: We need to set you some goals then. Can you be a little more specific about being fitter, for example, what will being fitter mean you can do that you can't do now?

Client: Oh, I've never thought of it like that. I guess I'd like to be able to go walking with my partner. He always complains that I'm too slow so I stay at home.

Practitioner: How long do you want to walk for?

Client: It would be good to be able to walk for a couple of hours – I get puffed after about 20 minutes at the moment.

Practitioner: So if we set a goal of walking for an hour without feeling puffed out, how would that be?

Client: That would be great, I'd love to get out with them on the local walk in the spring. It's just under two hours.

Practitioner: So if we set a short-term goal of being able to walk at a brisk pace for half an hour in four weeks to start with, how does that sound?

Client: Sounds good to me but how will I do that?

Practitioner: Start by walking for 20 minutes at lunchtime twice or three times a week and gradually build up the time and speed you walk at …

As discussed in Chapter 8, the focus should be on shorter, more achievable goals that look at behaviour rather than the endpoint. By building walks into everyday life, the client above is more likely to stick with it than if they have to make the effort to go to the gym.

## ACTION PLANNING

Forming an action plan is useful as it will help to identify any barriers and pitfalls that are likely to (and will!) occur and aid in planning ways to avoid or accommodate them. It will also ensure that the activity will be manageable within what is probably perceived to be an already full life.

Plans can relate to goals and be the steps needed to move towards their successful completion. They can be strategies to ensure time for activity is built into the day and to overcome barriers and pitfalls that will occur.

Examples include:

| Table 9.1 | Action planning |
|---|---|
| No time | Take ten minutes to walk, dance, stair-climb, do press-ups or squats each day. Do it once, twice or more but if you can only do it once, that is fine. |
| Feeling tired | Even a short bout of activity will help refresh and energise you. Tell yourself you will do five minutes and if you are still tired, you can stop – chances are you will want to keep going. |
| Family around | Do something with them so you all benefit. You can walk in the park, play with a Frisbee or see who can do the silliest dancing. |

Once the client is making changes there are other strategies that are useful, particularly in preparation for lapses or interruptions to routine.

## CONTINGENCY PLANNING

The best-laid plans usually get interrupted at some point. Relapse is common, especially after events such as holidays and Christmas. Putting strategies in place to minimise the interruption of these events will help to avoid relapse and may strengthen motivation so that the individual manages the situation and feels a sense of achievement at doing so.

| Table 9.2 | Common disruptions and some strategies to get past them |
|---|---|
| Christmas | Make time for activity during the day. Go for a long walk after lunch, dance to disco, have a race. Any activity that gets your heart and lungs working faster counts and will also help manage the stress that goes with Christmas. |
| Holiday | Holidays are our time to wind down from everyday stresses, however, swimming, dancing, walking, beach games or a pedalo are all fun ways to keep active. |
| Working away from home | Find a hotel with a gym or pool and use it. You can devise a mini-circuit using bands that can be done anywhere. |

## REINFORCE SUCCESS

Reinforcing achievements and success is important in keeping motivation going. One of the reasons for smaller goals is to be able to say 'I've done it' regularly, which will boost self-efficacy and keep the client going. Ensure the focus is on positive achievements and that any lapses are minimised or justified. This may be hard for some people as we tend to focus on negative aspects or any lapses, so it is important to get clients to focus on the positive benefits and successes so that they recognise these and also realise that lapses are normal and not worth worrying about. An example conversation might be:

Practitioner: It's been a few weeks since we had a chat, how have you been getting on?

Client: OK I guess, I've only managed to get to a class once a week though.

Practitioner: That sounds good when you consider that you didn't do that before, have you been doing anything else?

Client: Not really, apart from a lunchtime walk with a couple of workmates.

Practitioner: How many times a week do you go for a walk?

Client: Only two or three times for about half an hour, we don't really get time for a longer walk. It's sometimes hard to get to the class but I go because I like the instructor. She makes it fun.

Practitioner: She may make it fun but you are the one who gets you there each week so you deserve the credit for doing that. This is fantastic, you were doing nothing before and now you do something at least three times a week, well done!

Client: Gosh, I hadn't thought of it like that, I am doing well, aren't I?

The key here is getting the client to recognise and praise themselves for their achievements. A personal pat on the back is worth a lot.

## SUMMARY

Even if a client has been referred by their doctor for activity, the process of change still starts with the client and the initial conversation is an important factor in identifying how ready and willing the client is to make changes. From this, the practitioner can offer appropriate motivation and support at each stage of the process. Remember that sometimes clients are not ready, and that is fine. By initiating a conversation and offering a helpful listening experience, you have made contact and can leave the door open for them to return once they have considered their options.

### KEY POINTS

- Referral does not mean readiness.
- Clients are the focus of the process.
- All motivation is client-centred and finding the intrinsic motivation will help the client adopt and adhere to positive lifestyle changes.
- Communication skills are paramount to help the process along.

# MAINSTREAM SETTINGS

## 10

This chapter looks at the range of clients with whom a personal trainer or gym-based instructor may work. While an increasing number of clients are referred into dedicated exercise referral schemes, there are many who chose not to take this route but to find and work with a personal trainer or go to the gym. It is recommended that personal trainers or instructors who regularly work with clients with medical conditions, older adults or pregnant clients gain the appropriate qualification to ensure they have the necessary skills and knowledge and are insured.

The aims of this chapter are to:

- Review barriers to activity.
- Outline guidance for working with clients who are:
  - Overweight or obese
  - Pregnant
  - Older
  - Depressed or stressed

It is common for clients to join a gym, book sessions with a personal trainer or start attending classes with the aim of improving their health. It is equally common for this 'action' to be perceived as motivation, when in reality the client has only a vague idea of what they want, or can, achieve through activity. It is therefore important for personal trainers and gym instructors to spend some time in the initial stages finding out what the client's expectancies and motivations are as this will determine the success and maintenance of new positive lifestyle behaviours such as activity.

People who don't regularly access any activity give numerous excuses to justify their ongoing inactivity or sedentary behaviour, yet the reality is that most of these are just that – excuses not reasons. Clients make a choice, whether conscious or not, to be active or inactive and that is both their right and their decision. If a client really wants to change their behaviour, even the most significant barriers become manageable while, conversely, if they are not ready or willing to change then even the smallest excuses can be made to seem insurmountable.

Some common excuses for not becoming active include:

| | | | | |
|---|---|---|---|---|
| *No time* | | *Doesn't work* | *Don't like it* | *Too ill* |
| | *Too expensive* | | *No kit* | |
| *Too old* | | *No one to go with* | *Will get injured* | *Can't do it* |
| | *Not sporty* | | *Family commitments* | *Too fat* |
| *Too unfit* | | *Don't like getting sweaty* | | *Not that type* | *Too lazy* |
| | *No point* | | *Work commitments* | |
| *It hurts* | | *Tried it before* | | *Will miss the soaps* |

These may seem poor excuses to the practitioner but they are very real to the client and must be treated as such. At the root of these excuses is often a fear of the change; with activity it may be the fear of looking foolish, being the fattest/most unfit/oldest, not keeping up, getting hurt or just not being able to manage. With diet, it is often the fear of being left out, of failure or of having to give up something that is enjoyable! This fear may show as a sense of 'I can't …' and, as has been discussed, this may predict a poor outcome so an important element in the early stages of change is to help the client see that they 'can'.

## PERSONAL TRAINING

Personal trainers, whether working with clients in or out of the gym environment, have an important role in helping change as they usually work one-to-one and become trusted by their clients. Clients who employ a personal trainer are usually considered to be eager to see results and highly motivated – it is not a cheap fix after all! However, it could be argued that the need to employ someone to 'push' you indicates low motivation.

Personal trainers can employ the methods in this book to encourage their clients to become independent and confident exercisers who are working towards intrinsic goals with the support of the trainer, not the compulsion!

## WORKING WITH SPECIFIC CLIENT GROUPS

As discussed earlier, there are some client groups that need additional considerations, regardless of whether this is in a referral or mainstream setting.

### WORKING WITH OVERWEIGHT OR OBESE CLIENTS

The stigma of obesity and being overweight is still relatively high among fitness instructors and studies have shown a strong 'anti-fat' bias exists among fitness instructors and regular exercisers, particularly those who had never been overweight themselves (Robertson and Vohora 2008). Obesity and overweight issues were seen as a negative state that is within personal control and additionally perceived to be a 'self-induced' condition caused by a lack of personal control or laziness. Unfortunately, this means that obese clients may experience prejudice from the very people who could help them reduce and manage their weight. This is worrying as it may have taken every ounce of courage and determination an obese person can muster to come to an exercise environment and seek help and support in their weight loss programme, so the last thing they want or need is further discrimination and prejudice from an instructor. There may be many reasons for their condition, some simple and others more complex, but the only reaction they should receive is a welcoming, supportive one from you.

Unfortunately, this fear of being stigmatised or ridiculed because of obesity may prevent the client from seeking help and support in losing weight and becoming healthier. While an individual with diabetes or heart disease may expect (and will probably encounter) a great deal of support and understanding about their condition, the strong social stigma associated with obesity means that these clients may encounter negative attitudes, including perceptions of 'it's their own fault' or 'why don't they just eat less'. This is hardly likely to be supporting or motivating.

To help reduce fears and overcome any anticipation of stigma, it is important for the practitioner to show empathy and open communication and listen to the client without judgement or criticism. A tour of the facility at a time when there are others with similar body shapes, a discussion about some of the less complex or strenuous options, or talking to someone who felt the same way a few months ago but is now a regular may help. Discovering ways to include activity in daily life and finding an activity (possibly something from the past) that they 'can' do will also help to overcome fear – although it may take some time.

As with all goal-setting, it can be hard to divert an individual from an unrealistic, ideal goal focused on weight loss towards a more realistic one. Although this is essential if a successful outcome is to be achieved, it is particularly difficult in this area as a realistic weight loss goal may be significantly less than the individual's ideal loss and may deter them from even trying if they perceive it to not be worth it.

## WORKING WITH PREGNANT CLIENTS

Starting a regular activity programme is difficult enough for a sedentary client and when the less pleasant effects of pregnancy such as tiredness, anxiety, breathlessness and other symptoms are added, it makes it hard for the previously non-active woman to find the motivation to become active. However, there are a range of benefits of activity for all pregnant women who are able to exercise and most midwives now encourage participation as soon as the pregnancy is established.

It is recommended that any fitness professional or sports coach who will be working with pregnant women on a regular basis holds a recognised Level 3 qualification in ante- and post-natal exercise, and working with the midwife or other care providers is important. There are four broad exercise categories as shown in figure 10.1.

### The inactive pregnant woman

Any newcomer to exercise, particularly those who have been sedentary, requires their wants and needs to be discussed and a gradual progression of activity planned. A normally sedentary pregnant

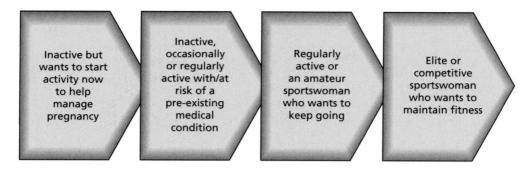

**Figure 10.1** General categories of pregnant exerciser (adapted from Coulson and Bolitho 2012)

client will need careful screening and assessment together with clear identification of goals as they may have unrealistic expectations around weight or fitness that would be inadvisable during pregnancy. Practitioners must focus on why the client wants to start to exercise now and what their motivation is and – if it is focused on an unhealthy outcome – may need to defer activity until a realistic expectation or outcome is agreed. In general, exercising when pregnant, at an appropriate intensity, is a positive thing, so the client should be encouraged to do so.

## The pregnant woman with health concerns or pre-existing medical conditions

While exercise referral instructors are used to working with clients with medical conditions such as heart disease, diabetes, obesity, arthritis or asthma, they may not have encountered these conditions in a pregnant client. Clients with the combination of pregnancy and a medical condition may decide to exercise to improve their general health or reduce risk factors during pregnancy or they may be regular exercisers who become pregnant. Generally, those used to exercise will

know how their bodies feel and will naturally taper intensity and volume of activity as the pregnancy progresses. However, as with all clients with risk factors or with a pre-existing condition, appropriate screening, risk stratification and goal-setting must be done at the start of the pregnancy, before activity either starts or continues.

## Regularly active or amateur sportswoman

Women who are regular exercisers and those who participate in sport may want to continue to exercise or train at a steady level through pregnancy. However, it is the responsibility of the instructor or coach to ensure that any goals or motivations are biased towards a healthy pregnancy and not to maintaining or improving fitness or performance.

## The elite or competitive athlete

Sports coaches working with elite athletes need to be aware of the physiological and psychological changes that occur during pregnancy and ensure that goals and training are appropriate. There are accounts of high-level athletes who compete very

| Table 10.1 | Task – process goals for pregnant women |
|---|---|

**Task**

Set some appropriate process goals for a pregnant woman based on the following aims:

| Aim | Process goal |
|---|---|
| I want to get back to shape within a month of delivery | |
| I want to keep attending my usual classes through the pregnancy. | |
| I want to keep training at my current pace throughout pregnancy. | |

close to delivery, however, this is the exception and not the rule, and an ethical coach will work with the client to develop a training plan that takes into account necessary changes to lifestyle and training to ensure a healthy pregnancy.

For all pregnant clients, maintenance of current fitness levels or as close to current as possible, is the key aim. Pregnancy is a time to focus on healthy lifestyle and behaviour and not to try to improve fitness levels so it may be necessary to employ some of the behavioural change techniques in Section 2 to develop appropriate habits and goals, particularly those related to weight gain. The average recommended gain in pregnancy is around 11kg or approximately two stone, however, this will differ with each woman and each pregnancy so there is no hard and fast rule about weight gain at this time. It is better to focus on slightly more vague goals such as:

- Keep weight gain close to recommended levels in each trimester.
- Maintain frequency of activity over intensity.
- Include posture reinforcement activities and exercise in each session.

## WORKING WITH OLDER ADULTS

Older adults are a growing population group and with life expectancy extending well beyond retirement age, many older adults are taking up activity to boost or maintain their health. Practitioners working with this client group need to understand both the physiological implications of ageing and the psychological issues that may arise.

Strong communication skills combined with a genuine interest in the client are essential when working with the older person (or, in fact, any client). Listening effectively and responding with empathy are also important. Consider the health and ability of the person before their age, many older adults are considerably fitter and healthier than those half their age and will probably be keen to maintain this health status and reduce the likelihood or effects of any medical conditions. Remember too that different ages of 'old' must be considered. Most instructors would not view or communicate with a 20-year-old client in the same way as a 45-year-old one, yet often the 'over-50s' are lumped together regardless of whether they are 55 or 80! Get to know your client and act and speak appropriately – you probably speak in a different manner when with your friends than

| Table 10.2 | Activities of daily living | |
|---|---|---|
| **Basic activities of daily living (BADLs)** | **Instrumental activities of daily living (IADLs)** | **Advanced activities of daily living (AADLs)** |
| Bathing | Light housework | Driving |
| Dressing and undressing | Preparing meals | Working |
| Eating | Taking medications | Travel |
| Transferring from bed to chair and back | Shopping for groceries or clothes | Gardening |
| Voluntary control of bladder and bowel discharge | Using the telephone | Exercise and physical activity |
| | Managing finances and budgets | Social activities |
| | Child-care | Religious activities |
| Using the toilet | Pets | |
| Walking (i.e. not bedridden) | Care of others | |
| | Community participation | |

with your grandparents so use this skill when working with older clients.

With most independent older adults, there will be a focus on maintaining independence and continuing to perform activities of daily living (ADLs). These ADLs are essential in maintaining an independent lifestyle and fall into three categories, basic, instrumental and advanced.

The independent older adult will, as the name suggests, be able to manage IADLs and most AADLs competently and live an independent life. Those adults who struggle with IADLs and BADLs, or who have a number of moderate to severe conditions or symptoms, may need additional care and consideration and instructors are advised to gain further qualifications to work with this group.

## WORKING WITH CLIENTS WITH MENTAL HEALTH CONDITIONS

This is a specialist field, albeit a growing one, and there are issues with behaviour change that are common with this population. For further advice on working with this client group it is recommended that an appropriate qualification is gained.

Adopting an active lifestyle can be challenging for many people, but factor in the symptoms of a mental health condition and compound this with the side-effects of medications and it is understandable that most people with mental health disorders are inactive, and there may be additional unhealthy lifestyle habits to contend with as well.

Where it is usual to relate change to an appropriate model, with this client group it is not particularly relevant as the effects of the condition or medication may reduce the capacity for insight into negative behaviours and affect decision-making about change. Clients may not understand the need for activity, or care about it. Any progression may be slow or non-existent, relapse is likely to be the rule rather than the exception and goals may need to be very vague (just to turn up may be enough) or led by the practitioner in the early stages (complete 20 minutes of activity when you do turn up). However, activity has a major impact on mental health (Lawrence and Bolitho, 2011) and is an increasingly recognised part of treatment. While an initial approach may just be to turn up, regardless of how much activity is done, once this is achieved, participation, time and intensity can increase as the confidence and comfort levels of the client increase.

## THE PROCESS OF CHANGE FROM THE PERSPECTIVE OF THE CLIENT

Often the process of change is outlined, discussed and agreed with the client, however, there may be emotions that occur which are worth considering. Fisher (2005) identified a personal model of change that may be useful for clients as it acknowledges a number of stages and emotions that may be experienced during the process of change (Figure 10.2).

1  Anxiety: Initial awareness of a need to change may lead to anxiety about the process combined with feelings of lack of control and an inability to see how the change will affect them.
2  Happiness: There may be a sense of happiness and relief that things are going to change for the better. However, it is important to ensure that this happiness is built on an accurate picture of the future, as people often assume that making one change will result in huge benefits, but this may not be the case.
3  Fear: There may be a sense of fear about making changes. Change often involves stepping out of comfort zones that may affect how the person sees themselves and how they feel others see them.
4  Threat: Not knowing how they, or others, will react to the change can feel threatening. For example, women who have lost a lot of weight often report that others (usually other women) behave differently towards them, perhaps seeing them as a 'rival' for the first time and this can increase fear of change.
5  Guilt: Making changes and becoming aware of past actions can give rise to guilt if they perceive past actions as having been hurtful or harmful to themselves or others.
6  Depression: While in the process of change, there may be a lack of motivation and clients may feel confused about the benefits of changing. There may also be a sense of fear about leaving the old self behind. This can lead to relapse and will need careful monitoring.
7  Disillusionment: Not seeing results quickly enough or feeling that you are out of step with others around you can lead to disillusionment, which in turn can lead to a plateau or drop in efforts. Sitting with a salad when others are tucking into pizza is enough to disillusion anyone!
8  Hostility: There is a saying that 'if you keep doing what you have always done, you will get what you have always got', and this is very true of change. Often people 'go on a diet' or take up an activity that has previously been unsuccessful in the hope that *this time* it may work. Any attempt to coach or guide towards new, lasting, behaviours will be ignored or undermined by the individual. The attitude is 'but I've always done it like this'.
9  Denial: Similar to hostility, denial is characterised by ignoring the impact of any change in behaviour. A short-term change in eating ('diet') resulted in weight loss and improved health or fitness so the goal has been achieved and the client can now return (back) to 'normal', effectively denying that the old behaviours were the cause of the problem.

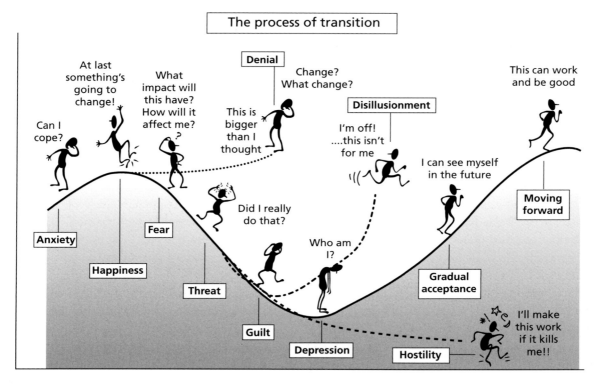

**Figure 10.2** Process of transition (John Fisher)

## KEY POINTS

- Not all clients are 'referred'.
- Change may relate to non-health goals.
- Transitions will vary between clients.

# BEHAVIOUR CHANGE IN SPORTS COACHING

11

Coaching has been described as 'the facilitation of behaviour change' as 'habituation applies not just to motor skills but the way we thing and attitudes formed' (Hadfield 2005: 36–7). An effective athlete must not only learn the skills associated with the game but also how to think and react appropriately within the sporting arena.

The coach has a vital role to play in encouraging individuals to take up a sport and in preventing drop-out. It is therefore important that the coach considers the style or model of coaching they will use. This takes on a greater importance as we see a move to encourage groups who may have been turned off sport in their youth to participate.

There are a variety of texts available on the coaching theory and the specifics of how to encourage skills development, but the focus of this section is to consider some of the factors that encourage long-term participation and adherence in sport and to provide some practical suggestions for coaches on how to create an environment that maintains athletes' motivation.

In Section 1, we described some of the factors (correlates) that are related to participation in physical activity. Many of these also apply to a sporting setting. Coaches need to consider how to make their sessions accessible to participants and to reduce any barriers to participation. It is also vital that coaches consider how to structure the sessions to ensure that they are fun, and provide an opportunity for socialising and mastery experiences, as these are key factors in encouraging long-term participation.

Another key element in encouraging participation is understanding motivational theory. Further information on motivation can be found in Chapter 4, but a key element that is important to the sporting context is how to give appropriate feedback. There is evidence to suggest that individuals who participate in sport in the long-term do so for predominantly intrinsic reasons, that is doing sport for its own sake, for fun or mastery (Biddle 1999: 127). There is also evidence that if extrinsic motivators such as rewards are used to encourage athletes, this could, in fact, harm intrinsic motivation (Jones et al 2008). Similarly the use of punishment – 'last one back does 20 press-ups' can also have an impact on motivation.

The use of appropriate motivators is of particular importance when working with children who, while competing in age-group categories, may be at very different stages of maturation. Traditional sporting competitions often reward the more mature athletes who are stronger and fitter due to their size as opposed to those who may be more skilful but are not yet as fast or strong. Performance reward based on growth levels may have a negative effect when it comes to encouraging long-term adherence, as it encourages individuals to focus on ego goals. Ego goal-orientated people measure success based on external and comparative factors, such as outperforming others, and therefore believe that ability is related to capacity. On the other hand, task goal-orientated people view success or ability as related to masterly, learning or skill development (Biddle 1999: 121). While being performance-focused is important in sport, there is a problem if the athletes do not believe that effort will lead to an improvement in their own ability – i.e. that only those with natural ability succeed – these people are unlikely to stay in sport. It is therefore important that feedback should be personal to the individual in relation to their improvement.

Another factor that can have an impact on the athlete's motivation is the ethos or style of coaching used. While a variety of coaching styles have been extensively described in literature, the coaching style that appears to be most effective in encouraging long-term adherence is a supportive, guiding or democratic approach. This style is characterised by:

- Athletes being engaged in decision-making.
- Interactive communication.
- Human values incorporated into goals and evaluation.
- The active involvement of the athletes in the learning process.
- Flexibility, empathy and support in personal relationships (Lyle 2002: 158).

The guiding style has been seen to be effective in encouraging participation but also in creating athletes who are more self-sufficient and able to perform more effectively.

> Athletes with supportive coaches show greater intrinsic motivation, enjoy participation and competition in sport and make more informed decision more rapidly in ever changing tactical manoeuvres and demonstrate trust is mutual.
> (Kidman 2005: 15)

A guiding style takes an athlete-centred approach and therefore the skills and techniques used will vary according to the situation and the level of development of the athlete. For example, it would not be appropriate to ask an athlete new to a sport to make tactical decisions in a competitive environment, and indeed would be setting them up to fail. The ultimate aim of using this style is to empower the athlete and therefore the coach would seek to move from a more coach-controlled environment to athlete-controlled one over a period of time (see Figure 11.1).

Previous sections in this book contain information that is relevant to the coach seeking to create a motivational environment that encourages long-term adherence (see Table 11.1), but in addition there are other specific actions the coach can take to develop an athlete centred approach.

1  Understand the athlete's motivation for participation – is it to be with friends? Is it to improve their fitness? – then create opportunities for these to be fulfilled.

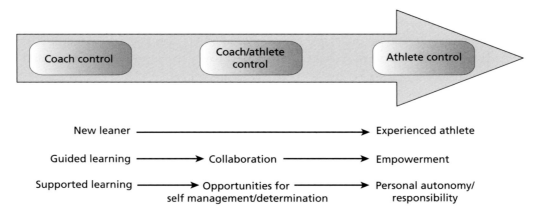

**Figure 11.1** Coach control and athlete control (adapted from Lyle 2002: 181)

| Table 11.1 | Creating a motivational environment |
|---|---|
| **Area** | **Section in book** |
| Models of change – especially those relating to motivation and self-esteem | Chapter 3 |
| Learning styles | Chapter 4 |
| Client-centred approach to working | Chapter 5 |
| Communication skills | Chapter 6 |
| Tools for behaviour change – especially self-esteem, goal-setting, calculating confidence, I-CAN | Chapter 7 |

2　Create opportunities for the athletes to be challenged and develop their skills, but not so far that they lose heart. Ensure that all participants are included in the learning experience; this may involve adapting the rules of the sport to take into consideration mixed abilities, and creating games that encourage cooperation and learning to occur.

3　Use both open and probing questions to understand the athlete's perspective but also to encourage thinking and learning.

4　Rotate roles to give participants a range of opportunities and experiences.

5　Praise individual effort and improvement.

6　Encourage athletes to evaluate their own performance.

7　Pay attention to how the athlete best receives information and learns, e.g. are they visual and learn through watching recordings or through writing notes/diagrams? Are they auditory and learn through instruction and verbal cues? Or are they kinaesthetic and need to feel the muscle movement to learn the skills? Perhaps they are a mixture of these? Try to ensure that you cater for different types of athletes' learning styles when providing instruction and feedback.

8  Use feedback to draw the athlete's attention and therefore reinforce best practice – this does not just have to be in terms of skills, but also in relation to attitudes and beliefs expressed.

9  Give athletes opportunities to take control of the game such as taking control over time-outs.

There is one last area to which the coach needs to give careful consideration and that is goal-setting. As part of the planning process of coaching, goal-setting is a vital element to ensure that athletes stay on track and hit performance targets for all stages of the planning cycle. The key to an athlete-centred approach to goal-setting is to ensure that the athlete is engaged in the process and is encouraged to take more control over the process. This can be done at an individual level and at a team level, and indeed supporting the team to develop some group goals may assist in increasing team cohesion. It is also important that some intrinsic goals are set, i.e. things that the athlete will accomplish or personal growth goals that they can achieve for themselves, alongside team and performance goals, to ensure that motivation is maintained.

## SUMMARY

Chapter 11 summarises the roles that coaches play in encouraging behaviour change. It focuses on specific considerations and argues the case for a guiding coaching style to encourage long-term participation in sport and gives tips on how to maintain athlete motivation

### KEYPOINTS

- Coaches have a key role to play in encouraging long-term participation in sport.
- A guiding and supportive coaching style is associated with long-term adherence in sport.
- Coaches should use techniques to encourage intrinsic motivation.

## FINAL SUMMARY

Change of any kind is not a simple linear undertaking, it can be spiral, undulating, stepped or messy and any practitioner working with clients in behaviour change will need to be flexible and adapt to the changing needs of the client. It can feel frustrating, irritating and even pointless at times, however, when clients manage to change, it is worth every moment to know that you have helped them along the way. For this reason, we recommend that those who want to make this field a large part of their work undertake training or gain qualifications in one or more of the techniques to help improve their way of working.

# REFERENCES

ACOG Committee (2002) 'Opinion no. 267: Exercise during pregnancy and the postpartum period', *Obstetrics & Gynecology*, 99: 171–3.

American College of Rheumatology (2002) 'Guidelines for the management of RA: 2002 Update', *Arthritis & Rheumatics*, 46: 328–46.

Ajzen, I. (1985) 'From intentions to actions: A theory of planned behaviour', in J. Kuhl and J. Beckmann (eds) *Action Control: From Cognition to Behaviour*, Berlin: Springer-Verlag.

— (1991) 'The theory of planned behavior', *Organizational Behavior and Human Decision Processes*, 50: 179–211.

Ajzen, I. and Fishbein, M. (1980) *Understanding Attitudes and Predicting Social Behavior*, Englewood Cliffs, NJ: Prentice-Hall.

Artinian, N. et al (2010) 'Interventions to promote physical activity and dietary lifestyle changes for cardiovascular risk factor reduction in adults', *Circulation*, 122: 406–41.

BACP (British Association of Counselling and Psychotherapy) (2010) *Ethical Framework for Good Practice in Counselling and Psychotherapy (revised edition)*, http://www.bacp.co.uk/admin/structure/files/pdf/566_ethical_framework_feb2010.pdf, accessed 26 December 2011.

Bandler, R. and Grinder, J. (1975) *The Structure of Magic: A Book About Language and Therapy*, Palo Alto, CA: Science and Behavior Books.

Bandura, A. (1977) *Social Learning Theory*, New York: General Learning Press.

— (1986) *Social Foundations of Thought and Action: A Social Cognitive Theory*, Englewood Cliffs, NJ: Prentice-Hall.

— (1989) 'Human agency in social cognitive theory', *American Psychologist*, 44: 1175–84.

— (2001) 'Social cognitive theory: An agentive perspective', *Annual Review of Psychology*, 52(1): 1–26.

Bauman, A.E. and Bull, F.C. (2007) *Environmental Correlates of Physical Activity and Walking in Adults and Children: A Review of Reviews*, London: National Institute of Health and Clinical Excellence.

Bayne, R. et al (1998) *The Counsellor's Handbook*, Cheltenham: Stanley Thomas Publishers Ltd.

Berne, E. (1975) *What Do You Say after You Say Hello?*, London: Corgi Books.

Biddle, S. (1999) 'Aherence to Sport and Physical Activity in Children and Youth', in S. Bull (ed.), *Adherence Issues in Sport and Exercise*, Chichester: John Wiley and Sons.

Biddle, S. and Mutrie, N. (2001) *Psychology of Physical Activity*, 2nd edition, London: Routledge.

Biehler, R. and Snowman, J. (1990) *Psychology Applied to Teaching*, Boston, MA: Houghton and Mifflin.

Boyes, C. (2005) *Need to Know? Body Language*, London: Collins.

Carroll, M. (2001) *NLP Practitioner Coaching and Business Skills Training Manual*, Croydon: NLP Academy.

Curzon, L. (2004) *Teaching in Further Education*, London: Continuum.

Davis, D., Kimmet, T. and Auty, M. (1986) *Physical Education: Theory and Practice*, Melbourne: Macmillan Education.

Davis, R., Roscoe, J., Roscoe, D. and Bull, R. (2005) *Physical Education and the Study of Sport*, 5th edition, Chatswood, Elsevier Mosby.

De Board, R. (1998) *Counselling for Toads*, London: Routledge.

Dickson, A. (1982) *A Woman in Your Own Right*, London: Quartet Books.

Donaghy, M.E. and Mutrie, N. ( 1999) 'Is exercise beneficial in the rehabilitation of the problem drinker? A critical review', *Physical Therapy Reviews*, 4: 153–66.

Dugdill, L., Crone, D. and Murphy, R. (2010) 'Physical activity and health promotion: Evidence-based approaches to practice', *Journal of Psychiatric and Mental Health Nursing*, 17: 1–8.

Duncan, L., Ghul, R. and Mousley, S (2007) *Creating Positive Futures: Solution Focussed Recovery from Mental Illness*, London: BT Press.

Egan, G. (2002) *Exercises in Helping Skills*, California: Brooks Cole.

Ellin, J. (1994) *Listening Helpfully: How to Develop your Counselling Skills*, London: Souvenir Press.

Erskine, R., Moursand, J. and Trautman, R. (1999) *Beyond Empathy: A Therapy of Contact in Relationship*, New York: Brunner Routledge.

Executive Coaching Forum (2008) *The Executive Coaching Handbook – Principles and Guidelines for Successful Coaching Partnerships*, www.executivecoachingforum.com/manuals/ECHandbook4thEdition032009.pdf.

Fava, J.L., Velicer, W.F. and Prochaska, J.O. (1995) 'Applying the transtheoretical model to a representative sample of smokers', *Addictive Behaviors*, 20(2): 189–203.

Feltham, C. and Horton, I. (eds) (2000) *Handbook of Counselling and Psychotherapy*, UK: Sage Publications.

Fishbein, M. and Ajzen, I. (1975) *Belief, Attitude, Intention, and Behavior: An Introduction to Theory and Research*, Reading, MA: Addison-Wesley.

Fisher, J.M. (2005) 'A time for change', *Human Resource Development International*, 8(2): 257–64.

Gilbert, A. (2001) *The Art of Making a Difference*, Reading: Cox and Wyman.

Gould, J. (2009) *Learning Theory & Classroom Practice*, UK: Learning Matters.

Grinder, J. and Bostic St Clair, C. (2001) *Whispering in the Wind*, Scotts Valley, CA: J&C Enterprises.

Gross, R. (1996) *Psychology. The Science of Mind and Behaviour*, London: Hodder & Stoughton.

Gross, R. and McIlveen, R (1998) *Psychology: A New Introduction*, London: Hodder & Stoughton.

Hadfield, D. (2005) 'The change challenge: Facilitating self-awareness in your athletes' in L. Kidman, *Athlete Centred Coaching*, Christchurch: Innovative Print Communication Ltd.

Harris, T. (1970) *I'm OK – You're OK*, London: Pan Books.

Harris, A. and Harris, T. (1995) *Staying OK*, London: Arrow Books.

Hayes, S.C., Spence, R.R., Galvão, D.A. and Newton, R.U. (2009) 'Australian Association for Exercise and Sport Science Position Stand: Optimising cancer outcomes through exercise', *Journal of Science & Medicine in Sport*, 12: 428–34.

Haywood, S. and Cohan, M. (1992) *Bag of Jewels*, Avalon, Australia: In Tune Books.

Hough, M (1994) *A Practical Approach to Counselling*, Essex: Longman Group.

Hunt, P. and Hillsdon, M. (2003) *Changing Eating and Exercise Behaviour: A Handbook for Professionals*, Oxford: Blackwell.

Ibrahim E.M. and Al-Homaidh, A. (2010) 'Physical activity and survival after breast cancer diagnosis: Meta-analysis of published studies', *Medical Oncology*, 28(3): 753–65.

James, M. and Jongeward, D (1996) *Born to Win*, Cambridge, MA: Perseus Books.

Jeffers, S. (1987) *Feel the Fear and Do It Anyway*, London: Arrow Books.

Jones, R.L., Hughes, M. and Kingston, K. (2008) *An Introduction to Sports Coaching: From Science and Theory to Practice*, Abingdon: Routledge.

Kidman, L. (2005) *Athlete Centred Coaching*, Christchurch: Innovative Print Communication Ltd.

Kram, K. (1988) *Mentoring at Work: Developmental Relationships in Organisational Life*, Lanham, MD: University Press of America.

Lawrence, D. and Bolitho, S. (2011) *The Complete Guide to Physical Activity for Mental Health*, London: Bloomsbury Publishing.

Leith, L.M. (1994) *Foundations of Exercise and Mental Health*, USA: Fitness Information Technology

Lewin, K. (1951) *Field Theory in Social Science: Selected Theoretical Papers*, edited by D. Cartwright, New York: Harper & Row.

Lyle, J. (2002) *Sport Coaching Concepts: A Framework for Coaches' Behaviour*, Routledge: London.

MacDonald, A.J. (2011) *Solution-focused Therapy Theory Research and Practice*, 2nd edition, London: SAGE.

McLeod, J. (2003) *An Introduction to Counselling*, 3rd edition, Buckingham: Open University Press.

Miller, N.E. and Dollard, J. (1941) *Social Learning and Imitation*, New Haven, CT: Yale University Press.

Miller, W. and Rollnick, S. (2002) *Motivational Interviewing: Preparing People for Change*, 2nd edition, New York: The Guilford Press.

Mind (2011) *Making Sense of Counselling*, http://www.mind.org.uk/help/medical_and_alternative_care/making_sense_of_counselling, accessed 27 December 2011.

Mindell, A (1995) *Sitting in the Fire: Large Group Transformation Using Conflict and Diversity*, Portland, OR: Lao Tse Press.

Nelson-Jones, R. (1995) *The Theory and Practice of Counselling*, London: Cassell.

— (1997) *Practical Counselling and Helping Skills*, London: Cassell.

NHS (2008) *Health Survey for England*, London: NHS Information Centre

— (2011) *Sport and Exercise Medicine – A Fresh Approach*, London: NHS Sport and Exercise Medicine Services.

NICE (National Institute of Health and Clinical Excellence) (2008) *The Care and Management of Osteoarthritis in Adults*, London: NICE Publications.

Orlick, T. (1980) *In Pursuit of Excellence: How to Win in Life and Sport Through Mental Training*, Champaign, IL: Leisure Press.

Pascal, E. (1992) *Jung to Live By*, London: Souvenir Press.

Peale, N.V. (1953) *The Power of Positive Thinking*, London: Cedar.

Pedersen B.K. and Saltin, B. (2006) 'Evidence for prescribing exercise as a therapy in chronic disease', *Scandinavian Journal of Medicine & Science in Sports*, 16 (Suppl. 1): 3–63.

Petty, G. (2004) *Teaching Today*, 3rd edition, Cheltenham: Nelson Thornes.

Phelps, S. and Austin, N. (1997) *The Assertive Women*, 3rd edition, Atascadero, CA: Impact Publishing.

Prochaska, J.O. and DiClemente, C. (1983) 'Stages and processes of self-change of smoking: Toward and integrative model of change', *Journal of Consulting and Clinical Psychology*, 51(3): 390–5.

Prochaska, J.O. and Velicer, W. F. (1997) 'The transtheoretical model of health behaviour change', *American Journal of Health Promotion*, 12(1): 38–48.

Prochaska, J.O., Norcross, J.C. and DiClemente, C.C. (2006) *Changing for Good*, New York: Collins.

Puhl, R. and Brownell, K.D. (2002) 'Stigma, discrimination and obesity', in C.G. Fairburn and K.D. Brownell (eds) *Eating Disorders and Obesity*, New York: The Guildford Press, 108–12.

Reece, I. and Walker, S. (2003) *Teaching, Training and Learning*, Oxford: Business Education Publishers.

Rinpoche, S. (1992) *The Tibetan Book of Living and Dying*, London: Rider.

Robertson, N. and Vohora, R. (2008) 'Fitness vs. fatness: Implicit bias towards obesity among fitness professionals and regular exercisers', *Psychology of Sport and Exercise*, 9: 547–57.

Rogers, C. (1969) *Freedom to Learn*, Columbus, OH: Charles E. Merrill.

Rogers, C. and Stevens, B. (1967) *Person to Person: The Problem of Being Human*, Lafayette, CA: Real People Press.

Rollnick, S.R., Miller, W.R. and Butler, C.C. (2008) *Motivational Interviewing in Health Care: Helping Patients Change Behavior*, New York: Guilform Press.

Rollnick, S.R., Manson, P. and Butler, C. (1999) *Health Behaviour Change: A Guide For Practitioners*, Edinburgh: Churchill Livingstone.

Rosenstock, I.M. (1966) 'Why people use health services', *Millbank Memorial Fund Quarterly*, 44: 94–124.

Sanders, P. (1997) *First Steps in Counselling*, Ross-on-Wye: PCCS Books.

Spirduso, W.W., Francis, K.L. and MacRae, P.L. (2004) *Physical Dimensions of Ageing*, Champaign, IL: Human Kinetics.

Steiner, C. (1997) *Achieving Emotional Literacy*, London: Bloomsbury Publishing.

Stewart, I. and Joines, V. (1987) *TA Today: A New Introduction to Transactional Analysis*, Nottingham: Lifespace Publishing.

Sunderland, M. and Engleheart, P. (1993) *Draw on Your Emotions*, Oxford: Speechmark Publishing Limited.

Taylor, R.S. and Brown, A. (2004) 'Exercise-based rehabilitation for patients with coronary heart disease: Systematic review and meta-analysis of randomized controlled trials', *American Journal of Medicine*, 116: 682–92.

Trost, S.G., Owen, N., Bauman, A.E., Sallis, J.F. and Brown, W. (2002) 'Correlates of adults' participation in physical activity: Review and update', *Medicine and Science in Sport and Exercise*, 34(12): 1996–2001.

Waine, C. (2002) *Obesity and Weight Management in Primary Care*, Oxford: Blackwell Publishing.

Wallace, S. (2005) *Teaching, Tutoring and Training in the Lifelong Learning Sector*, Exeter: Learning Matters Ltd.

Wallace, S. and Gravells, J. (2005) *Mentoring in Further Education*, Exeter: Learning Matters Ltd.

Zinker, J (1977) *Creative Process in Gestalt Therapy*, New York: Vintage Books.

# WEBSITES

British Association of Counselling and Psychotherapy (BACP) www.bacp.co.uk

United Kingdom Council for Psychotherapy (UKCP) www.psychotherapy.org.uk

Coaching Chartered Institute of Professional development (CIPD) www.cipd.co.uk

International Coaching Federation (ICF) www.coachfederation.org.uk

European Coaching Institute www.europeancoachinginstitute.org

European Mentoring and Coaching Council www.emccouncil.org/uk

Institute of Leadership and Management (ILM) www.i-l-m.com

Executive Coaching Forum www.executivecoachingforum.com

# INDEX